OUTHOUSES

OUTHOUSES

Roger Welsch

MBI

This edition first published in 2003 by Motorbooks International, an imprint of MBI Publishing Company, Galtier Plaza, Suite 200, 380 Jackson Street, St. Paul, MN 55101-3885 USA

Motorbooks International titles are also available at discounts in bulk quantity for industrial or sales-promotional use. For details write to Special Sales Manager at Motorbooks International Wholesalers & Distributors, Galtier Plaza, Suite 200, 380 Jackson Street, St. Paul, MN 55101-3885 USA.

ISBN 0-7603-1637-6

Front Cover: © *Richard T. Nowitz/CORBIS*

Senior Editor: Darwin Holmstrom
Associate Editor: Peter Schletty
Editorial Assistant: Mariam Pourshoushtari
Designed by Joe Bonyata

Printed in Hong Kong

For Mick the Brick

Contents

Roger Welsch

Author's Note

My purpose in these pages is not simply to produce a work about our toilets and outhouses nor even to effect a return from the toilet to the outhouse (although that is clearly and admittedly my subtext here!) but also to provide a volume that may come to be seen as a part of the outhouse. To those ends, as it were, the publisher considered printing the book on absorbent, soft, textured paper and has provided a punched hole in the upper left-hand corner of the book to facilitate its easy hanging for ready access in a traditional outhouse. Or if it must be, in a conventional modern toilet. Unfortunately we were unable to locate a print shop capable of conforming to these specifications.

For my own part, I have tried to write this book in sections suitable in length to reading and digesting in one sitting, as it were. The traditional outhouse is a place of comfort and ease, with the understanding that here, of all places, there should be no rushing of the processes of nature . . . indeed, here there should be time for the contemplation and appreciation of the wonderful ways in which our metabolisms serve us. To that end, so to speak, I have tried to keep the sections of my text comfortably sized to match the reader's best course for the beginning of the process, taking small, easily digested bites of a fine meal, slowly, appreciatively, chewing each bite politely and thoroughly. Let this slim volume be equally suitable to the mind and bowel alike.

Introduction

"For this relief, much thanks...."
—William Shakespeare
Hamlet, act 1, scene 1

I've never understood why so many scenes in movies, novels, and plays focus on events in the bedroom when the fact of the matter is, the bathroom is the most interesting room in the house. No room in the house is furnished with quite so many unique and curious items as the bathroom. A bedroom in Paris is, well, a bedroom. It has, for example, a bed. But a bathroom in Paris can be almost anything but is very likely to be a substantial departure from what you have grown up with considering your standard bathroom equipment in Sheboygan, Wisconsin!

To be sure, there are regional differences in the *salle de bain* in America, or at different economic levels. On a couple occasions I have been a guest in some pretty tony hotels in major American cities, for example. The sleeping area is fairly standard: a bed with sheets and a cover, maybe twin beds; a bedside table with a telephone, a clock, and a lamp; maybe a desk, maybe a table. Sometimes there is a couch, sometimes a recliner, perhaps only a chair. There is a longish, largish dresser of sorts with drawers, maybe a television set perched atop it. That's pretty much it. Not a lot of surprises there.

Outhouses

But now let's take a look into the "private room." Why is it that some hotels consider a shower cap a basic freebie, while others do not? Why does one Holiday Inn provide me with body lotion, and another thinks I should have a shoe polishing cloth instead? Shouldn't we pretty much have the fundamental showerhead standardized by now? So why are there big ones that gush and little ones that squirt, and throbbers and stingers and drippers? Why are there sometimes two faucets to adjust and on others only one? Why do we sometimes push for water, other times pull, or turn, or twist? And couldn't we all agree on how to turn the water from the tub spigot to the showerhead?

And what is this here? A magnifying glass with a built-in light? And a hair dryer? Okay, that's nice, but what is this I see here? A telephone? Who got the idea of putting a telephone by the toilet? I don't want to talk to anyone while I'm, well, you know, and I don't want them talking to me at that delicate time either, and to be perfectly honest, I am almost absolutely certain no one wants to talk with *me* while I am indisposed, as the phrase goes, so what I am really curious about is, who does use the phone whilst seated on the throne?

On second thought, maybe I don't want to know.

And what's the deal with the little envelope fold at the end of the toilet paper? Is that for something? If so, I don't know what it is, and I just don't feel comfortable asking the young woman at the front desk. After you use paper, are you expected to put that little fold back in the paper for the next person? Toilet seat up, toilet seat down? Throw used towels on the floor, fold them neatly in the corner of the vanity top, hang them back on the rack? Do you get to take all the little freebies—sewing kit, shower cap, body lotion—with you even if you don't use them? Will the lady who cleans the room notice that the hotel shampoo is gone, but there is no empty shampoo container in the bathroom wastebasket? Will she think less of you if you take it with you, rather than using it in her shower?

We don't even know what to call these places that are so necessary that they have in our recent past been called a "necessary." Ladies' room, men's room. How's *that* for a locution? Why ladies but not gentlemen? *Rest* room? Is *rest* a really good term for what we do there when often it actually requires no small effort? Powder room? Little boys' room? Relief station? Pit stop?

What's more, some of us have our doubts about the multitasking we, at least we Americans, have brought to this, the smallest room of our home, pooping, bathing, brushing our teeth, storing our medicines, performing morning and evening ablutions, applying makeup, in some motels and hotels making coffee, for Pete's sake, and—please, dear Lord, let it be—reading. No wonder there is a tacit theory that personalities are formed and shattered here. No one says, "He is a very rich man because he once had a couple weeks of problems in the bedroom, if you catch my drift, in his younger years, so he's never gotten over it and he therefore drives his employees like sled dogs to make up for this momentary lapse of vigor." No, but people do say, "Yeah, sure, he's rich, anal retentive you know." No further explanation needed. We all know what that means, and we all know where it happened. Or, as the case is, didn't happen. "He must have been a real problem in potty training."

I know what is happening at this very moment—your mind is flying from one of your acquaintances to another, probably to your employer, as you acknowledge that bathroom behavior or nonbehavior is a solid determinant for later personality development. Our bathrooms then are a good deal more than small spaces set aside for putting aside. Yes, our toilets are places where heroes and villains of our societies are made and broken; they therefore deserve far more credit and attention than we have given them, anthropologically, philosophically, spiritually, intellectually, poetically.

And that's what I'm about to do in these pages. This is not simply a book about outhouses, however, or even about elimination. This is a book for reading in your outhouse, but is also an apology and appeal for the return, refurbishing (in both architecture and reputation) of not simply the outhouse in its more restricted manifestations but of the privy in its more general manifestations too, whether that be a New York hotel bathroom—a windowless, sterile, uninspiring, echoing, cold place of little comfort, or that wonderfully airy, open, natural, inviting, friendly, sheltering comfort of the rural chapel. Brought to my own farm outhouse by the gentle urgings of my metabolism, about which I promise you will read little more in these pages, I have devoted some considerable time to thinking about the meaning of life and man and outhouses and a thousand other issues, which I now present to you.

Why the outhouse? Why not my shop, which has after all inspired a half dozen other books? Why not the living room of our home where I spend many hours within the bosom of my family? Why not the kitchen, which is the real heart of any genuine American home? Or the patio? Or, certainly more logically, our automobile? Well, because I do my most and best philosophical thinking in the bathroom, inspired by a daily bathroom reconnection with my fundamental nature—my basic humanity, and the time to consider it. And this is a book of essays thus inspired.

No matter how frantic our days, no matter what problems beset our families, no matter how oppressive our associations with other human beings or nature, no matter what, there comes a time when we are required by our very most basic natures to stop, sit, and, like it or not, relax. And inevitably, to think. The essays in this little book result from my own musings during my daily moments of introspection, and my sincerest hope is that you will read and consider them during yours. In a way, this book is an experiment in communication. Perhaps in these moments of mutual identity, we, you and I, will understand each other better than at any other time of our day, any other moment of our otherwise very different lives.

Roger Welsch

Despite all the clichés, laughter is not a universal language; around the world we laugh at very different things, and sometimes, cruelly, at each other. Food is certainly not universal. We gag and retch when confronted with what other people eat, and they condemn us to hell for eating the most vile of foods, forbidden by various and sundry gods. Music is not only not a universal language, the howling and whining my beloved wife Linda calls music is enough to bring me to emptying a shotgun into a radio—even a car radio. Beauty is not international, not even spanning the gap from one generation to another.

Is there anything we humans do that we universally share, that we all do, that we all do pretty much the same, that we all find comfort and relief in, men and women, young and old, regardless of religion, nationality, or race? Of course there is. We all poop and pee. And we all poop and pee fundamentally in pretty much the same way—fundamentally. Perhaps in this small niche, mankind can at last be brought together in a renewed kinship. Language, religion, sex, customs, those things all separate us, but maybe in the communality of the irresistible geologic pressures of yesterday's supper—be that bean curry or Cajun gumbo or Minnesota lutefisk or a peanut-butter-and-jelly sandwich—we are all brought to the same place and put in the same position—seated—in a bathroom. Pretty inspirational, huh? Talk about a "fellowship of man!" No matter how different we are at any other point along our alimentary canal, when it comes right down to it, as it were, we are fundamentally, so to speak, the same.

While that union of man is true in terms of the process, the preference of venue for that process is not so universal. I have conducted a scientific survey of upward of two dozen modern, living human beings who have used an outhouse, and the results are dramatic and conclusive: most men figure an outhouse is just fine (although men are generally pretty much content to do their alimentary leavings wherever the spirit moves them, including in public places) while women

6

universally would rather just hold it for a week or 10 days, rather than use an outhouse. Now that I think about it, that may be one of the very reasons men find an outhouse so inviting—in an outhouse there are few women, which also means there will be no rappings at the door in midrelaxation, no wet panty-hose hanging in the immediate area of the front-row seating, no diaper buckets sending forth their distinctive reekings, no discomforting thoughts about what is happening below you while your toothbrush hangs only a yard away, no medicine cabinets clogged with vials insisting that the contents be used up before the end of World War I, no makeup kits, no hair tints, shampoos, conditioners, body emulsifiers, split-end menders, root stimulators, follicle refurbishers, dandruff tonics, highlight refreshers, luster enhancers, blah, blah, blah. . . .

Thus, the male species—and men and women are indeed separate species no matter what misguided biologists may think in this matter—is not only driven from the in-house relief station by the overwhelming occupation and influence of his female counterpart(s), he is welcomed to his outhouse by their parallel absence there. Man, is that a tidy paradigm, or what?

Nope, an outhouse is, as the book by Chic Sales so long ago made clear, a place of specialization. One poops and pees in an outhouse. And does some reading and thinking, of course too, but that's about it. It's a place where a man can enjoy his solitary thoughts, a perfect literary irony, the most spacious and free room of the homestead, and yet by far and away the smallest. There surely is a poetic message there somewhere.

Besides, the outhouse has traditionally been the place for the forbidden mysteries. Archaeologists love locating ancient outhouses, because long-gone clients of the little buildings saw them not simply as relief stations for evacuating the bowels but also for lubricating them. An ancient privy pit is a great place to find ancient liquor bottles, stashed out there by the Old Man, emptied, and then discarded deep into that dark recess where the Little Lady would never look, no matter how bright the sunshine. (To be perfectly honest, however, the frequency of finds involving high-alcohol elixirs for "female complaints" suggest that many of our grandmothers also found the outhouse a convenient place for indulging one's appetites.) More by accident, old privy pits are also the archaeologist's favorite place to look for lost firearms; the process seems obvious: a pistol carried loosely in the pocket falls easily out and with the unerring certainty of a dropped toothbrush goes inevitably down the hole and deep into the morass below.

Same with the lingerie section from the Sears catalog or the *Police Gazette*, which could be stashed out there in the outhouse and examined with delicious care. Even today my own outhouse has a tin box, originally a kitchen bread box, I think, in which I keep some extra reading materials, if you catch my drift, a couple Swisher Sweet cigars, and a small flask of Jack Daniel's Black Label Tonic for Gentleman's Complaint. But don't tell Linda. She doesn't know about such things.

1
Form and Format
of the Private Place

I already told you that this is not going to be simply a book about outhouses, so what do you think I'm going to start off talking with you about? Yep, outhouses. I think that before we move along to the philosophical, we should plant our feet firmly in realities, and in the case of this little book, that would be the outhouse. I feel the need for this chapter in part, I suppose, because I am betting not one reader in 1,000 will actually read it in an outhouse. And such a shame that is. But 40 years ago I wrote several articles on a form of traditional plains pioneer architecture, the baled-hay house, and it caused such a stir, was reprinted so many times, and gathered in so many readers who wanted to try this unique and extraordinarily efficient housing form for themselves, that I started something of a baled-hay revival. Now baled-hay buildings are popping up everywhere. And small wonder: They were a good idea a century ago, and they're still a good idea today.

Maybe this same revival of interest will happen with privies. So maybe while you sit in a library or living room or winter retreat in Akumal reading this, I am writing it in my cupola-capped outhouse on the open plains of Nebraska. And perhaps my example will shame or inspire you to at least consider building a relief retreat of your own—your own outhouse. That would be nice. I would consider that a tribute.

Location, Location, Location

Okay, let's start with where you are going to put your privy. Not so close to the main house that it could be a constant embarrassment, not so far that a trip there is a burden rather than a comfort. I recommend that you give this not only some thought but even some practical experimentation. Find out what is a comfortable stroll for you when the inspiration strikes, so to speak, by placing yourself some distance from a toilet and then slowly but surely lengthening that distance until it becomes a clear discomfort to get there. Obviously, the progressively longer distances should be taken in small increments, and with some attention to your own schedule and eating habits.

In the old days a family privy was often sited close to the hog house or chicken coop, even between the two. The idea was that embarrassing odors coming from the outhouse would fade to total insignificance when juxtaposed with something as noxious and evil as a hog lot, or chicken coop, or both, and human frailty would thus merit nary a mention. I think the comfort of the occupant transcends the sensitivity of the casual passer-by, and that an outhouse should therefore be placed with priorities for visual aesthetics and accessibility. Besides, hasn't anyone thought about how offended the hogs and chickens might be?

Place your outhouse in such a way that it is not in the central view from your living room picture window. Or kitchen.

Outhouses

This is why tradition dictated that the outhouse be set not directly out from any one side of the house, but in a line drawn through any of the two opposite corners of the house. This ensures that the little building will always be at the extreme edge of the view from any of the house's windows or doors. Neat, huh?

If it is at all possible, I place my outhouses facing south so I can enjoy the sun on my knees, an especially welcome warmth during the winter. As noted elsewhere, I have a large picture window at my right hand in my own outhouse, facing the trees and hills of my central Nebraska Sandhills tree farm. I have known people who place their outhouses to catch the early morning sun (for much the same reason as I prefer the south) or the west to take advantage of the beauties of local sunsets. It almost makes one wish for an outhouse on a turntable, doesn't it? I cannot for the life of me imagine a single reason to face an outhouse to the north and don't know that I have ever seen one with that orientation, other than the one mentioned below that was cantilevered out over a deep creek bed; that particular environmental atrocity could serve us all as a model for bad outhouse placement.

It is best to put the outhouse on the same elevation as the house, but if you must deal with an incline, make your trip to the biffie a downhill one, and the trip back up the hill. You don't want the strain and effort of climbing a hill on your way there, especially if you are in something of a hurry. Or if it is snowy or muddy and slick going. I don't think I really need to go into detailed explanations here, do I?

Outhouses were often placed behind a copse or bush to hide them discreetly, and often near another outbuilding or facility like a woodpile, thus providing double duty for the daily trip. Go to the outhouse—gather the eggs. Go get firewood—go to the outhouse. That kind of thing.

Consider your water source when locating your privy. Again, you wouldn't think this would require a lot of explanation, but I am told that the old Danish settlers in these parts piled manure up around the pump during the winter so the natural warmth of the organic breakdown within the pile would keep the pipes from freezing. I don't think this is a good idea and may account for a lot of the peculiar mental aberrations I see around here with depressing regularity. Once in Tennessee I saw an outhouse, I'm not kidding here, built on a rickety platform out over a pleasant little creek, thus eliminating the problems of ever having to dig a new hole but, I would think, causing some concern for the folks who lived about 200 yards down that same creek bed. I think putting our eliminations back into the earth is a pretty solid idea, philosophically and hygienically. Pooping directly into a watercourse, on the other hand, offends aesthetically. Doesn't it?

Your privy should be oriented with its door away from the house and paths of frequent commerce, but when I place my own outhouses, I also consider the view. I'm going to be spending some time here, after all, and I want to look out on something pleasant and inspirational. My own principal privy (as opposed to the lesser facility near our cabin down by the river) has a lovely picture window facing the open prairies to the west, so even if I close the door discreetly, I look out on my estates. Lovely Linda once, in an effort to civilize the barbaric, made lovely flowered curtains for that window, but nature struck back and declared its preëminence when grasshoppers ate them within the month.

Swing In, Swing Out

One of my favorite American writers is Wright Morris, who is famous as an art photographer as well as a novelist. Morris grew up just down Ormsby Road from me, over by Central City, about 25 miles to the east. There's a reason why it's to the east. When I was looking for a piece of ground whereon to plant my feet and soul, I gave serious thought to Morris's description of the landscape I most admire. He started his novel *Works of Love* with the words "West of the 98th meridian, where it sometimes rains and it sometimes doesn't. . . ." I love those words for some reason, maybe because I know that the 98th meridian is actually 17th Street, running smack through the middle of Central City, about 100 feet east of where Wright Morris grew up. So, when I was looking for some ground, I looked west of the 98th meridian, because I like questions much better than answers.

One of the joys of my life has been that I have been in a position now and again to meet and talk with people I admire, especially writers I admire. One of the best evenings of my life was eating a long, leisurely, delicious supper sitting between Charles Kuralt and Calvin Trillin. Beat that for dinner company! Anyway, I also had a chance to spend some time with Wright Morris. And so I got to ask him my deepest, most intense, philosophical questions about his work. Like, what the hell does it mean that the door on the pictured outhouse in his book *The Home Place* (pages 84 and 108) opens in rather than out? I've never been seated in a single outhouse in my entire life that opens in rather than out.

Well, Morris' explanation did not let me down. I was surprised not only that he knew the answer but also that there is an answer. (I'm trying to build up some literary tension here by holding back from telling you that answer just as long as I possibly can.) Morris explained that, sure, private privies open outward, that in fact, a lot of outhouses in his own long rural experience would have fallen over on their faces if the door had not been open and holding them up. (By now you must be dying to know why that door in Morris's photo opens in, huh?) Thing is (here it comes) public outhouses should open inward . . . so you can hold them shut with a foot while you are in there! Isn't that great?

More from Wright Morris later on. There's a man who knew his outhouses, inside and out.

4
A Firm Foundation

I feel foolish telling you what should be obvious, but there should be a solid foundation and a receiving hole under your privy, and I would hate to have you miss the importance of that basic factor. I'd feel foolish taking up your time with this idea, except for my late and much lamented friend Rod Hat, who had something of a reputation in our little town during his life for simply moving his privy and setting it at various places around his home without bothering to dig a hole. This practice has more drawbacks than I really want to discuss here.

I have built wooden boxes for privy "basements," thinking that the box would eventually rot away leaving almost no sign that I had been there, many times, as a matter of fact. But in my later sloth, I have simply dug the hole and placed an open-top 60-gallon barrel in it. Our soil here is very loose, mostly sand, in fact, and without some sort of container, the sides would quickly fall in and put me roughly in the same class, privily speaking, as Rod Hat. Some people punch holes in the bottoms or sides of the barrel, thus providing a kind of drain field, but I think you will be pleasantly surprised at the amount of poop a 60-gallon drum will hold, and you will not soon find yourself having to dig another hole for yet another barrel. There was a time when great pride was taken by the householder in his skills at digging a privy pit that would stand up to the demands of time. My town of Dannebrog,

Roger Welsch

Nebraska, is a very Danish town. The name Dannebrog is the romantic Danish name for their flag—the oldest flag in the world, handed down to the Danes in battle by God! So many of the traditional tales around here are couched in a Danish accent. I guess the accent doesn't make much difference in the following story, but, well, that's the way I've always heard it, so that's the way I always tell it.

Lars, Gunnar, and Rass were drinking a little once and got into an argument about who could dig the best outhouse pit. Lars said, "Me, I digs a hole and den I puts de outhouse over it, and den I goes in and sits down. And I do vat I needs to do, and I start counting—vun, two, tree, four, five—and only den does I hear it hit the bottom of dat pit, ker-plop." There is a moment's appreciation for the magnificence of a privy pit like that but then Gunnar says, "Vell, me, I digs a hole and den I puts de outhouse over it and den I goes in and sits down. And I do vat I needs to do, and I start counting—vun, two, tree, four, hundert, two hundert, ten hundert—and only den I hears it hit de bottom of dat pit, ker-plop." Another few minutes of contemplation and admiration, but then Rass says, "Vell, me, I digs a hole and den I puts de outhouse over it and den I goes in and sits down. And I do vat I needs to do, and I start counting—vun, two, tree, four, hundert, two hundert, ten hundert, four tousand, a million—and only den does I notice, damn, hung up in my overall straps again, like always."

It's not so funny. Overall straps and privies have a long and not always happy relationship in precisely the way parodied in that tale. Many overall manufacturers, in fact produced "low backs," overalls with buttons on the straps at the back, which allowed the visitor to the outhouse to pull his straps up from behind and drop the seat of his overalls without those dangerously loose and dangling straps right where they do not need to be during a procedure largely emanating from precisely that location.

5
Nor Walls a Prison

You wouldn't think there'd be much to say about the walls of an outhouse. I mean, well, you know, walls. But you'd be thinking wrong. There is a reason they say, "She's built like a brick shithouse," and I have seen both stone and brick outhouses—great places to be during a tornado or atomic attack. (You never—never—hear anything about terrorists flying airplanes into high-rise privies.) But the most interesting privy variation I have heard in this category is something called a "Michigan outhouse." I have never seen one myself, so the precise specifications remain something of a mystery, but it seems like a good enough idea that someone probably has indeed built such a thing. As I understand it, the privy is built with both an inner and outer wall. The space between the walls is filled in the autumn through a slot in the top of the inside wall with dried cobs and then, during the winter, the cobs serve first as insulation against the ferocious northern winter, and cobs are pulled out from a slot in the bottom of the inside wall to be used as, well, to be used, if you know what I mean. Thus, in the spring, when you are ready for a refreshing breeze to waft through your "private place," the cobs are gone and the walls are open again to some ventilation.

6
Diversions

A good outhouse, providing as it does its own diversions, doesn't need much more than this. And perhaps some good reading material. I usually have an old, inexpensive set of encyclopedias in my outhouses—adds a bit of class as well as an abundance of reading material—but I am currently between encyclopedias. (Hopefully this volume will correct a similar deficiency in many another outhouse.) I keep a copy of the current *Old Farmer's Almanac* not only in my outhouse but also at my bedside and even at the couch in our front room. There are simply too many occasions when one needs an almanac to have to run out to the outhouse to fetch the family's one and only copy. (By the way, is it really true that for years the *Old Farmer's Almanac's* meteorologist was the unfortunately named Dick Head?)

I have an indoor and an outdoor thermometer in my outhouse, and some nice art prints on the wall, although I rarely look at them, I'll have to admit. I mean, jeez, winter = cold, summer = hot. What with an encyclopedia, men's magazines, and a picture window, I can't imagine what other diversions a man would want during his visits to the outhouse. Except maybe for a gun.

7
Forewarned Is Fore-Armed

My wife, Linda, once used the toilet (indoor) of Flora Sandoz, sister of Nebraska author, pioneer, and tough cookie Mari Sandoz. To give you some idea of what kind of woman Flora was, I was once going to talk with her about something or another literary, which is saying more than you might imagine (1) if you don't know that she lived in the heart of the Nebraska Sandhills (the largest sand dune area in the Western Hemisphere), (2) if you don't know how utterly bleak the Sandhills can be, and (3) if you don't know that she lived many miles down a "road" that was little more than two sand-bogged ruts crossing willy-nilly over and around the dunes and hills. That is to say, it was quite a jaunt to "go to talk with her about something or another literary. . . . "

On that occasion I was worried about disturbing this nice old lady, well up in her 80s at that time, too early, so I asked her if 9 A.M. would be suitable for my arrival. Okay, yeah, sure, it was going to take me two hours to get to her ranch house from the nearest place that had anything resembling a motel, but still, I really was thinking of her health and happiness too. I didn't need to. She said, "Okay, I'll be coming in for a break from haying about that time anyway." And as I drove up, sure enough, she was just coming in from the hay meadows on her tractor.

After her first visit to Flora's bathroom, Linda came out with a wry smile on her face. "Uh, Flora," Linda asked, "why is there a loaded shotgun in your bathroom?"

Flora's answer says as much about toilets as it does about her and the Sandhills: "Just in case." We didn't inquire any further.

8
Another Argument for the Second Amendment

I would keep a gun in my outhouse if it weren't so hard on the gun—the rust and dust and all. I used to have what I would consider a perfect indoor bathroom if you have to have an indoor bathroom. What was nice about it was that it was very small, which means I could reach just about everything, but best of all it was on the second floor and had a big, low window right in front of the toilet. That's one of the things I hate about hotel bathrooms: no windows. I suppose that's so no one can look in, but I can't help but wonder why no one has noticed that that also means no one can look out.

The best bathroom I have ever visited in this regard is in the vacation home of my friends Verne and Terri Holoubek in Akumal, Mexico. The shower is situated in a building extension out from the main wall of the house so that three of its walls are full-length windows. Yes, yes, yes, people can look in, but don't forget, *you* can look out! And there is nothing but beach and ocean and sky. It is the most luxurious shower I have ever enjoyed. And the toilet is situated just outside the shower so you can pull back the curtain and have the very same view even when you're not taking a shower.

But where was I? Oh yes, my indoor bathroom in Lincoln. Well, I spent a lot of time sitting there looking out over my back yard, the garbage men emptying barrels in the alley, my dog lounging in the sun, the neighbor's damn Siamese cat strolling across the yard yowling a complaint at every step if my dog Slump were inside, and therefore barking insanely through the window, wishing he were outdoors killing that cat, and of course the squirrel that took enormous pleasure in coming down a huge elm tree in my yard and stopping just one inch above the high-jumping capability of Slump, thus driving him even further into the insanity Squirrel's partner-in-crime Siamese cat was doing his part to enflame.

Well, I enjoy some peace and quiet when I am in the bathroom. I don't like yowling cats, chattering squirrels, and barking dogs. This cat and squirrel were striking deeply into my own repose and contentment. This by way of excusing myself to those of you who might be cat or squirrel lovers, although frankly I find it laughable that I should be the one making excuses to you! I bought a pellet gun. A really good pellet gun. Not a Red Ryder Special. "Sportsman's marksmanship with riflelike accuracy," it said on the box. And I put it up in my bathroom, right beside the window, in front of the toilet.

Nothing much happened for a few days and I wondered if maybe I had wasted my money, but sure enough, about six days after I had armed myself in my castle keep, I was sitting there relaxing, reading something elevating no doubt, when I heard the yowl of that damn cat. And there he was, strolling across my yard, complaining at every step, and paying not the slightest bit of attention to Slump, now barking madly at the kitchen screen door. I swallowed deeply and for the first time in my life felt what the hunter calls buck fever. I knew this was my chance, perhaps my only chance. I don't have a lot of experience with guns. And certainly not with this one, although I had plinked a little bit in delicious anticipation of this very moment.

I picked up the air rifle and checked it over quickly . . . safety off. I leaned slightly forward—my, uh, reason for being there restricted somewhat my mobility—and I aimed. And I fired. The result was more explosive than I could have imagined. That cat went 15 feet straight up in the air and looked for all the world like one of those startled cats in a Booth cartoon in the *New Yorker*. I exploded in laughter. It was incredible. The cat hit the ground with his feet churning, his disdainful contempt, his cool disregard now totally shattered, and to his surprise and mine, not three feet in front of a free-charging Slump, who in his own enthusiasm at my marksmanship had torn through that screen door like it was those paper things high school football players run through as they come running onto the field.

In three gigantic leaps, howling like an air-raid siren, the cat hit the top of our fence and launched himself a good 25 feet into the neighbor's yard and its safety from Slump's now-insane fury. Now, you have to understand that I am already in this fraction of a second reduced to a complete laughing breakdown from the total collapse of this arrogant feline's aplomb, Slump's declaration of his freedom to life, liberty, and the pursuit of Siamese cats, the vertical launch of that cat, the leap to the fence. . . .

9
Wait ... There's More!

This splendid event unfolding before my delighted eyes wasn't over. The neighbor's chocolate Lab was always so good-natured, so easy going, that while he would have enjoyed chasing that damn cat any day, good or bad, he just never managed to get up and about in time, or he was busy chewing on a bone, or maybe he was taking his sun bath, whatever the excuse, he always showed interest in that cat but never enough to do anything about it.

Until this moment. The howl of the cat's vertical launch, the noise of Slump breaking through that door and chasing him in full halloo across the yard and up that fence had finally stirred Hershey, the chocolate lab, to action, and his timing was exquisite. (Remember: I am watching all of this from the perfect seat of a second floor toilet and large, low window!) The cat hit the neighbor's lawn approximately 3.3 inches in front of Hershey's nose and unlike Slump, who had started with the handicap of a dead stop and was still carrying fragments of my screen door around his neck, Hershey was unfettered and moving almost exactly as fast as the cat as he came off the fence.

A cat can do amazing things in a situation like that, and this Siamese cat did what he had to. I have never seen any animal move that fast, in such magnificent parabolas. I'm not kidding you, he landed on the roof of the next neighbor's garden shed. I never saw the cat again. He wasn't hurt—you can't hurt a cat like that—but he couldn't help but hear the roars of laughter from me, not to mention Slump and Hershey, and he just couldn't bear to face that kind of humiliation and disgrace again. I wouldn't be the least bit surprised to hear that that cat went home and hanged himself from a Venetian blind cord later that very same day.

10
Where a Man Can Play God

But that wasn't the end of my adventures with a gun in the bathroom. About as quickly as I realized that the cat was never again going to give me the pleasure of igniting a feline space launch in my own backyard, the squirrel that loved vexing Slump took on his tormenting assignment with new determination. He came ever farther down that tree until, so help me, as he hung there upside down on the tree trunk, his nose couldn't have been more than a quarter-inch above the highest extension of Slump's nose. I came to hate that squirrel like I had never hated the cat.

But I knew how these things can go now and so I was patient. I waited for the perfect shot. I let the squirrel build up his confidence. I worked on my own marksmanship. I actually put a target on the tree about where the squirrel did his ugly daily exercise in doggy torture and practiced until I could hit it with every pellet. And finally the day of reckoning and revenge came.

Now try to understand: I am an animal lover, a strong supporter of the Humane Society, no hunter, but just as there are bad people who need to be removed from society, this damn squirrel had gone too far. It was not me who was taking pleasure in inflicting pain and misery on animals, but *he* and his incessant torturing of poor Slump, a good dog who would have preferred to spend his entire life lounging in the sun, thinking about the days before his operation.

Roger Welsch

There I was, again on the toilet. And Slump was going crazy. And that squirrel was just hanging there, chattering, teasing. There was no other legitimate reason for him to be there, hanging fractions of an inch above Slump's nose. The squirrel was having one grand time tormenting a perfectly good black dog. Until that perfectly aimed pellet hit him. He was surprised for the remaining instant of his life, but not nearly as surprised as Slump. The squirrel died instantly, still hanging there upside down above Slump's nose, and then he dropped. Right into Slump's open mouth. Slump stood there in total silence, utterly stunned. I like to think that for just one moment he felt he had been touched by the hand of God, and in a way he had after all. He stood there another moment. He shook the dead squirrel, then dropped it and stepped back to look at this wonder that had been delivered to him as mysteriously as the tablets were delivered to Moses on Mount Sinai.

But Slump's moment of awe and worshipful silence almost immediately passed to unbridled glee, a fulfillment that over the years he had come to believe would never happen. He picked up that squirrel carcass and pranced around the yard, throwing the corpse into the air and catching it before it hit the ground. He shook it with the fury of years of frustration and torment. He growled and barked and bit and chewed and at the end of the day not a tooth, not a toenail of that wretched late and unlamented squirrel remained.

I never tried to explain to Slump what had happened that day. I thought he should continue to live with his own belief of how that justice had come to be served. All I know is that I was one happy dog owner that evening, and Slump was one happy black dog. Thus, while firearms are not a necessary component of your outhouse's fixtures, you may want to give the idea some thought. Besides, what happens if the Commies attack while you're sitting there reading the latest issue of *Playboy* and contemplating the wonders of the universe? You need at least a pellet gun.

11
It's Not Done until the
Paper Work Is Finished

Inflicting justice is not the only way I have enjoyed being a *deus ex machina* for the animals around me. I have also learned a few birdcalls—that of the bobwhite, blue jay, cardinal, peewee, meadowlark, and cardinal, for example—and sometimes amuse myself while relaxing in my outhouse by starting up a conversation with the various birds around me. I have actually lured blue jays within arm's length. In an outhouse it doesn't take much to enjoy oneself. Try calling a blue jay in your indoor toilet! (I'll have to admit that my conscience has bothered me however with such bird calling; I can't help but wonder if maybe I'm not imitating a female making all sorts of libidinous promises and suggestions, and then just when I get the male all heated up and ready for a good time, he discovers it's a fat guy in overalls sitting in the little house on the hill. I know how I'd feel in a situation like that.)

The entertainment potential of a well-situated, well-appointed outhouse can be a problem. John Schweizer told me a story he heard at his mother's knee, well, actually in a recitation she did for a talent night at a church summer social in Illinois long ago. He said, "Outhouse design was a topic of much conversation not long ago. Seems that the hired help would lose track of time while sitting on those carefully contoured wood planks, basking in the sun coming through a slightly open door, reading a few select pages of the Sears catalog before putting them to their appointed use.

Well, grandfather solved this problem by putting square edges on the holes and replacing the paper supply with corn cobs of two different types: red for the work and white for finishing (and, as the story often goes, to see if you need another red!). Thus visits to the outhouse became strictly business in nature and short at that."

I am reminded of the time my friend Dee went into our small-town grocery store—very small-town—and complained that there wasn't any yellow toilet paper to match the décor of her bathroom. Steve Hoke, then-manager of the store, explained, "Dee, we sell it to you white. You make it yellow."

Cobs have to be the most misunderstood wipe of all time. I know what you are thinking—everyone thinks that—but cobs are actually quite soft and downy. And talk about "quilted!" Cobs have to be the most efficient tool for this purpose ever devised. If we want to be offended, let's consider those parts of the world where one uses one's left hand to perform this function. I don't care how careful you are with that left hand, I don't want to deal with anyone whose culture moves, so to speak, in this direction.

The bidet-type bathroom furniture that uses a water jet for cleansing might conceivably be a worthy advance, but hey! This book is about outhouses, and water jets are not, strictly speaking, appropriate to the discussion. The closest you'll come to this kind of thing in an outhouse is when a flurry of winter snow blows up through that inevitable crack under the back of the outhouse, the one you swore you were going to fix last fall. Toilet paper is, however, something of a problem in the traditional outhouse. And I'm not talking about that inevitable toilet philosophical question from the Martha Stewart set about whether the paper should issue from over the top of the roll or out from the bottom. It should be perfectly clear to anyone: It must come over the top.

The big problems with toilet paper in an outhouse are legion. First, it is a perfect place for bugs, especially spiders. Although I am not nearly as goofy about bugs and spiders as my wife and daughter, nonetheless, I do not care to deliver a brown recluse or black widow spider directly to the seat of my affections, if you know what I mean. Secondly, just as toilet paper is soft and cushy for your tushy, it is the perfect lining for pink little baby mice, so the discriminating Mommy Mousie will shred any exposed toilet paper she can find to construct a lovely layette for her next litter, leaving you a tattered roll of lacy frills, fancy and lovely but scarcely suitable for its intended purpose. So I keep the paper in my outhouse in a closed coffee can. It works perfectly: right size, right shape, very tidy.

One of my favorite examples of the immense wisdom of our Native American forebears is the Omaha system for infant waste management in their earth lodges. The Omaha had permanent villages along the banks of the Missouri River, where it now borders Nebraska and Iowa. The huge semisubterranean lodges each housed between 30 and 50 people comfortably, so there were always babies crawling around the house. Now, you can't just have naked babies crawling around your living quarters pooping where they will. So here's what the Omaha did: They had large, soft skin pillows, which they filled with soft downy cattail fluff in the fall, making a kind of beanbag chair, perfect for lounging around the fire. Unhousebroken babies wore light deerskin diaperlike seatcovers lined with cattail fluff, as soft and gentle as any commercial diapering material we have today. As a child soiled the lining, it was removed and discarded. The adult in charge reached into the large pillow, pulled out another handful of cattail fluff, relined the diaper cover, and turned the kid loose to crawl around in comfort. Isn't that amazing? The Indians had beanbag chairs and disposable diapers. And the pioneers called them "savages."

12
The Feng Shui
of the Outhouse

It's not that I don't accept the principles of *feng shui*—I just don't know much about them. I know that it is an ancient and venerated Chinese system for organizing one's environment in a way that is best suited to deal with the positive and negative forces of the universe around us. And who's to say it doesn't work? Not me!

There have been many millions of people over the centuries who have sworn by feng shui, and many today who to one degree or another accept or follow its principles. In an unobtrusive, nondogmatic way, my wife Linda counts herself among their ranks. I have asked Linda to give some time and energy to considering the Feng Shui of the outhouse, a consideration I don't believe has been previously explored. Her observations follow.

Feng Shui for Outhouses
By Linda Welsch

Our grandparents had it right. On rural farmsteads across America our forbears located their outhouses a discreet distance from the main house. This is very good feng shui (pronounced fung shway). Feng shui is the ancient Chinese art of situating your physical environment in such a way as to enhance chi, which is positive energy flow and harmony (see figure 1).

Outhouses

Unfortunately modern convenience puts many of us at risk of depleting our life force by having bathrooms in our houses and apartments. First, the good energy of our house can literally circulate down and away through the bathroom. Secondly, the somewhat iffy chi (energy) of the bathroom can permeate the rest of your house, negatively affecting your life and wealth. For an enjoyable read and solutions to this sticky wicket, look for the book *Feng Shui for Dummies* by David Daniel Kennedy.

For those of us lucky enough to still have an old, if unused, outhouse on the premises, it's time to reclaim these outbuildings and bring them back into the family. It is part of our landscape and our heritage.

First, fling the door of the outhouse open on its one remaining good hinge. Do this on a bright sunny day so you can get a good look at what you're dealing with. Remove old issues of the *National Geographic* and anything else that's not waterproof. Power wash the inside of the outhouse with a hose and sprayer to remove spiders, cobwebs, and dust. Let dry thoroughly while you take a long look at the approach to the outhouse. Weedy? Overgrown? Think about bricking the pathway, planting flowers, and repairing the roof. A fresh coat of white outdoor paint with a good working door and latch would be a lovely and positive energy change.

Spruce up the interior with one of the new pastel shades of Martha Stewart paint and add some bright color accents. Keep toilet paper clean and dry in an antique metal tin and add a plant for good chi. In this instance, an artificial plant works as well as the real thing, requiring only a minimum of care. In our outhouse, we have a working window. If you're also lucky enough to have one, add a window shade and a curtain swag for a homey touch.

Although not usually done in bygone days, it is also good feng shui to have a cover over the holes to the "mysterious below." When my aunt Arlene was little, she fell down the hole and was covered with enough bad chi to last a good long while.

Roger Welsch

The small configuration of most outhouses causes several problems you may want to mitigate. If the "sitting" area is located along the back wall, there is a potential problem in that this area corresponds to the wealth, fame, and marriage areas (see figure 2). Again, it is good to have a proper lid or cover over the openings to counter the potential drain of these life areas. To cure the negative energy of seeing the elimination area of the outhouse immediately upon entering the door, hang a faceted crystal sphere from the ceiling halfway between the door and the sitting area. Hang it by a red ribbon that is nine inches long for an extra boost of good energy.

Provide a little shelf inside at the left front to hold reading material. This area corresponds to the knowledge area of this small room, so bring back the *National Geographic,* add some catalogs and James Johnson's Horse Feathers cartoons. On the right front side, you might want to add another small shelf to hold the plant and a candle in a jar. This corner corresponds to the Helpful People section of the room and especially correlates to the wellbeing of males in the household. It is important not to reverse these two areas. If you are situated inside (once again, coincidentally in the Fame area) looking out, the front right-hand side is the Knowledge area, and the front left-hand side is the Helpful People area. Placing a throw rug in an earth color at your feet will positively reinforce the Health area.

If you happen to be one of the truly lucky or blessed living on a rural homestead, take a moment to admire this little outbuilding. You can sit inside your private outhouse at dusk, the door flung wide open (who's to see?) with a candle burning in the cool evening air. Can there be a better way to enhance harmony and positive energy flow in your life?

Outhouses

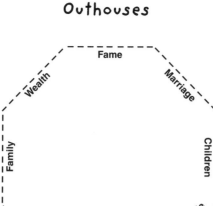

Figure 1 The feng shui octagon is a visual tool you can use to divide any living space into life areas. The theory is that you can improve your life by improving the corresponding areas in your living space.

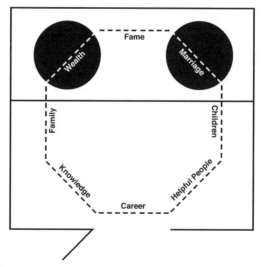

Figure 2 The octagon superimposed over a typical outhouse with a center door. [Author's Note: Now, see what I mean? That's what happens when a woman takes control over an outhouse. Feng shui. Curtains. Martha Stewart paint. Chi.]

13
An Outside Chance

Perhaps one of the reasons the proper outhouse is more acceptable to male than female occupation is that men can deal with at least one of the processes of organic elimination with no physical structure being necessary at all. And it is further my clear impression that men, given a choice, would rather pee on the ground (or variously against a tree) than bother with any porcelain or wood targets at all. It is more than convenience, too. Ask any honest man and he will tell you that peeing outdoors is akin to William Wallace's (a.k.a. Mel Gibson) primal cry in the movie *Braveheart*: "*Frrrrreeeeeeeeeddddddooooommmmm!*" Peeing outdoors is a primal male declaration of manhood, of oneness with nature, of the unfettered, feral primate.

For many years there was a small, dingy, country tavern not far from here, pretty much the main building in a tiny village at the edge of the Nebraska Sandhills. The woman who ran this tavern lived in it too, so it was for all the world like stepping into a slightly disreputable aunt's living room and enjoying a couple of drinks with her and whoever of her boozy friends happened to be there at the time. One of the main attractions of this place was its toilet facilities. Or more specifically, its facility for male visitors, because other than being pretty seedy, the ladies' room was otherwise conventionally porcelain.

Outhouses

It was a favorite practice for locals to take visitors, especially visitors from the city (which in central Nebraska means any town with more than 1,000 inhabitants) to this wide spot in the road for a drink. Or two. The goal was to pour enough beer into the greenhorn to get him to ask the lady in charge where the men's room was. She would growl and point toward a plain board door at the back of the one-room tavern. Then everyone would laugh as the visitor opened that door—especially if his needs came after dark and he stepped through the door without seeing what lay before him—and found himself outdoors, under the day's sun or the night's stars.

Because that's what you did here—peed right there on the ground, up against the back fence, just as men have done for a million years before you. If it was good enough for Og, it is good enough for you.

Thing is, men would be surprised, then chagrined at the laughter of their friends, and then, in my judgment at least, relieved. In both ways. Psychologically and physically. It was, everyone agreed, much more pleasurable to pee into the open air than to use a urinal, even considering the fun of chasing a cigarette butt or fragment of urinal cake around with a stream of relief. Men are meant to pee outdoors. Only a pervert calls it "indecent exposure."

14
Biblical Defiance

When Lovely Linda and I first became an item, I lived at a fairly respectable house (respectable considering that I had been a bachelor for a few years) in Lincoln, Nebraska, but had a wonderful, ancient log house here on my piece of land down along the beautiful Middle Loup River of Central Nebraska. One of the reasons the cabin was—and still is—a wonderful retreat is that it had no modern "conveniences." (I will explain something more about those skeptical quotation marks a few pages down the road.) There is a very nice WPA outhouse about 50 paces through the woods out the cabin's back door, but even that journey through the snow, dark, rain, or cold was not a real burden since it was only necessary once a day. Maybe twice on a good day. The rest of the time I just stepped out the front or back door, marched a respectable couple paces farther, and peed at will. I could do that even with bare feet in the snow . . . a minor discomfort at worst.

The only problem arose when there were women guests. And eventually Linda became much more than a guest; indeed, she became the hostess of this lovely, if basic, shelter. Some women readily, but rarely eagerly, grasp the notion of leaning up against a tree or car door in order to affect a quick and easy position of relief, but Linda never mastered this technique, even when it was not a matter of "dipping it in the snow." I tried my best to explain to her that as uncomfortable, even humiliating, as this might be, it was after all, biblical. It was woman who had brought this on herself in the Garden of Eden by violating God's injunction against sampling of the Tree of Knowledge. I understand that there may be some scriptural scholars who disagree with my interpretation but frankly, to me, it seems fairly obvious.

Linda endured this divine punishment for a year or so. I stepped outside, peed quickly, and came back into the warmth of the house while she waded through the snow and faced the dark, the hooting of owls, the howling of coyotes, the ticks and snakes, and the skunk that for some years lived under the outhouse. Perhaps the worst of it was my laughter at her discomfort and my constant reminder that this discomfort was after all the result of a perfidy of, well, of biblical proportions.

Then one day Linda threw the very foundations of Judeo-Christian theology to the wind and bought a chamber pot. Now, not only did I have to step out into the cold and snow, dark and beastie-infested world to relieve myself while she pees in grand comfort and warmth inside, now she also made me step out into the cold and snow, dark and beastie-infested world when she felt the need to pee. My exit on these occasions occurred because this was a very small, one-room house and Linda has what she characterizes as a "shy bladder." To this day, every time she uses that chamber pot down there I can swear I hear the voice of Moses (a.k.a. Charlton Heston) scolding us for deviating from the will of God.

15
Roughing It

There are some delights of peeing al fresco (I almost wrote al dente!) that neither the chamber pot nor outhouse can provide. And I don't think that men simply like to pee outdoors because they can and women don't because, while they can, it is not quite as elegant. (My son Chris once advised a young lady in our company simply to assume a three-point stance. She was not amused.) I think it's a matter of marking territory, like a dog, coyote, elk stag, or elephant bull, if I might boast just a little. I will sometimes make a deliberate effort to forestall a pressing urinary need until I get home to my own territory, not simply because I am a male, not simply because I am a child of the Great Depression and don't like to throw away anything, but because I see my small role in the grand scheme of things and do what I can to help my fellow man.

Here is my theory: We live on the banks of the Middle Loup River in Central Nebraska, high on the western watershed of the enormous central plains and prairies of the North American continent. We are in a marginally farmable region on the constant edge of severe drought. So here's what I do to help out humanity, nature, America, and you. I drink Heineken, St. Pauli Girl, Wisconsin beers, sometimes Kansas City or St. Louis brews when those climes are beset with flooding. That is, I do what I can to remove water from areas where water is a problem. Sure, it's a small gesture in the face of enormous problems but if everyone did this, the people on the dikes and levees, filling sandbags and rescuing the near-drowned would be damn grateful.

But that's only half of the equation. Next, I make a point of getting back home before, well, before it's too late, and I pee in my backyard. I am thus not only taking water from where it exists in excess, but now I am moving it to water-deficient areas. I pee in my backyard, watering our trees, shrubs, flowers, and grass. But the benefits do not end there. That water seeps down through the prairie sands and soils and before very long reaches the water table beneath us and the river water not 300 yards to our south. Then that Dutch, German, or Wisconsin water goes downstream through Nebraska, along the way being taken out by pumps and diversions to water crops to grow the food that feeds the world. Then it reenters the river and goes farther downstream where it drives turbines to make electricity for the towns and villages. It enters the Platte where it provides water for sports and recreation, for wetlands, and for wildlife along thousands of miles of banks and bayous, and then it reaches the Muddy Missouri where it cools the seething rods of atomic power plants, and on, on, on to the Mighty Mississippi, where it floats barges carrying crops, cars, lumber, and steel to New Orleans, and finally out into the Gulf of Mexico and on, on, on to nations all around the world. From the oceans of the world it is lifted once again to the skies to fall in Holland, Germany, Wisconsin, and Missouri to provide millers and brewers with the pure waters they need to make their malty elixir. There the brewers remove water from the excess inventory that afflicts their countrymen and countrysides, starting this marvelous circle of life spinning once again.

So, when I hoist a cold one, I see it not as a matter of personal pleasure but as a fulfillment of my cosmic obligation. The world needs more men of responsibility like me.

16
More *Plein Air* Artistry

I'm not alone in finding joy in the incredible freedom of the *plein air* whiz. I once hosted a several-day-long New Year's Eve party at the log house down by the river. It was wonderful. The snow was deep—we had to wade through a good quarter-mile of waist-deep snow to reach the place, dragging our provisions behind us on sledges and toboggans. It was bitterly cold, which only enhanced the glow of the wood stove, and the fellowship was thoroughly warm.

Two events come to mind in the spirit of this book. First was the morning I went out to relieve myself in the shallower snow behind some frozen lilac bushes when I spotted several trails of little tracks in the snow. This sort of thing has always interested me. There are thousands of wild creatures, from howling mice (I'm not kidding) and wild turkeys to mountain lions and coyotes living down there in the river woods, and only in the snows of winter could we see that they had visited us silently in the night, where they had gone, and what they had been up to. Even these little bird or mouse tracks were curious, tracing mysterious runes in the snow.

I called my friends out from the cabin and invited them to help me guess what sort of creature had made the tracks and what he had been doing. The guess ran from birds—chickadees looking for small grass seeds perhaps—to prairie voles. We could only guess, none of us having the expertise to give anything close to a definitive answer. Only when we turned to

40

Outhouses

go back to the cabin and saw the goofy grin on my buddy John Carter's face did we realize that we had been duped. Yes, the tracks were indeed evidence of an untamed night spirit, but in this case it was only John, full of beer the night before, trying to write his name, or perhaps the Declaration of Independence, in the snow with his own urine.

17
John Again, As It Were

I think it was that same weekend that John regaled us with stories of his famous huevos rancheros (the entire story and his recipe appear in my book *Diggin' In and Piggin' Out*) and then revealed that he had brought along all the ingredients to produce the same the next morning, which to make things even more agonizing was New Year's Day, which is to say, the waking moment after New Year's Eve. As I have told you, this cabin consists basically of one room (and a partial loft) measuring 18 by 20 feet. So when one person of a 10-person party starts banging pans and dishes (not to mention whistling some sort of random twittering that was for all the world an audio version of what he had peed in the snow only 36 hours before), there is no escape. You are not only a witness to a predawn cook's enthusiasm—like it or not, you are a part of it.

Well, it was worth it. John's huevos were terrific: eggs, milk, peppers, hot sauce, just the thing for a deep winter gathering of a party of friends. We all ate the dish enthusiastically and praised John without restraint. After all, how could we have known what was yet to be visited on us? None of us spoke Spanish so we had no idea that *huevos rancheros* translates as *gastric nuclear device*.

It didn't take long. And you could hear it before you could feel it. Stomachs starting growling and a few members of our party laughed at the poor souls whose insides seemed

Outhouses

tormented to the point of crying out for escape. But then the laughers began to feel the same seismic tremors. And it wasn't long before the first of John's victims made the long, cold, snowy dash to the outhouse. And then another. And then, even before the return of the last departure, another of John's victims left the house. And then the line started at the door, and as soon as a good eye could see the outhouse door begin to open, the next tortured soul set out, the two thus meeting at a halfway point between the cabin and the outhouse. Well, not actually a halfway point because those leaving the cabin and heading for the outhouse were traveling a good deal faster than those returning.

I'll have to admit that as pained as I was by my own gastric imitations of Mt. St. Helen's, I genuinely worried about the welfare of my old friend John. Not that he had eaten twice as many of his own napalm neutron devices himself, but that the crowd was getting uglier and uglier as the line got longer and longer and as the morning dragged on. Frankly, the only thing that stopped what was turning into an angry lynch mob was that every single member of that mob had something much more urgent on his or her mind than lynching John at that particular moment.

Today, some 25 years later, I don't think a single person has ever again eaten anything cooked by John Carter.

18
Where Is the EPA
When We Need It?

I can imagine some conscientious young modern turning up a nose at the notion of spreading human feces all over the countryside. Well, there are some reasons to believe that is a far better notion than concentrating it all in one place and thus creating a massive toxic dump that really requires special attention and concern. Poop is biodegradable, after all. And it is more degradable in tiny amounts than in massive amounts. The problem may not be where we poop as how many of us are pooping in any given place.

As I write these words, cities around me are flailing wildly because of a lack of the most basic material for life, human or otherwise: water. Nebraska is blessed with an abundance of clean surface water and an ocean of subsurface water in the form of the Ogallala aquifer. Endless supplies of water, both above the ground and under it.

Well, uh, we thought it was an endless supply. But all at once we are running out. What's worse, we are not simply running out of water, we are polluting what water we have with leaky fuel tanks, spilled explosives at abandoned military sites, agricultural chemicals, on and on. Sizable cities are buying water in gallon containers. Others are developing restrictions for using water for frivolous purposes like watering lawns or washing cars, limiting toilet flush tanks to cut down on the millions of gallons of water wasted with every single flush of every toilet in any community per day. Finally, some areas are taking steps to protect individual well heads from pollution.

But consider the outhouse, a small, personal septic system that allows human wastes to break down into harmless organic materials slowly, in small amounts. Here's the best part: Calculate the amount of water used by your average outhouse user per day. One user, times, oh, say, three visits per day—let's say one big stinky and a couple number ones—times rock-bottom zero water usage, square your hypotenuse, carry your six, apply your Pythagorean Theory, mass times the speed of light squared equaling something or another, and you get, let's see, carry the naught, yep, just as I suspected, zero! The water consumption in my own humble outhouse per year is maybe two gallons, which is what it takes to do the spring and fall cleaning. You throw away many times that much water every time you flush your toilet for a whiz you could just as easily have performed behind a tree in the back yard, you miserable polluter, you.

19
A Celebrity's Tale

Dick Cavett is an old friend of mine. He and I graduated from high school together. I'm sure he won't mind me telling this story about him, even if his behavior in it is disgusting, disgraceful, humiliating, illegal, disrespectful, and certain to alienate the affection of many of his fans who think he is such a sweet young man, so clever and well spoken. Maybe just to be safe I should use an alias to protect him. Yeah, that's what I'll do. Forget everything I've told you about Dick Cavett.

I want to tell you a story about another guy I know, Rick Davit. Yeah, Rick Davit. He's pretty famous from his work with national television, having, uh, worked as a gaffer on several soap operas, most notably *The Young and the Restless*. Anyway, Rick came to visit me one evening but showed up too late for Linda to cook anything, so Rick and I went to town. Well, we found that the grill was already closed at the tavern so next we drifted over to Harriett's Danish Café, where we noticed the lights were still on in the kitchen and there seemed to be some traffic out in the eating area.

We went to the back door to avoid bothering whatever was going on inside and to avoid Dick, uh, "Rick" being troubled by folks who might recognize him and want to tell him about ideas they had for their own soap opera scripts. Harriett was astonished when she opened her back door and found the two of us there, but she whisked us inside, put us at a table in the kitchen where we wouldn't bother the wedding rehearsal dinner going on in the front of the café, and where they wouldn't bother us. We had a grand supper of roast beef, mashed potatoes, gravy, salad, and some of Harriett's famous Danish bread.

As Harriett always does when distinguished visitors come to her kitchen, before we left, she dragged a bottle of Aquavit, a Danish vodka, lightly flavored with caraway or dill— "Aquavit" translates into English as "water of life," by the way—and literally forced us to throw down a couple shots. It goes down so easily when it is frozen and then ignites about the time it hits your liver.

Well, it turns out that Dick, er, Rick doesn't drink much. Aquavit is rough stuff even on the experienced, jaded drinker, but it can really be hard on the amateur, so the walk back down the now-dark main street of Dannebrog was a long one, aggravated by the fact that Dick (to hell with the alias) felt the increasing urge, pressure, requirement to pee, and I mean now.

We made it as far as the post office before there was no longer a choice for poor Dick. We were only a dozen steps from my pickup truck, but Dick made it clear that he didn't have a couple more steps in his bladder, and that was all there was too it. So, he stepped up to the wall of the post office and peed. Honestly, he didn't mean it as a sign of disrespect to our nation nor the U.S. Postal Service. It was the action of a total innocent unable to do otherwise.

I got him back to my place and settled in for the night, and the next morning I took him back up town for one of Harriett's famous Danish pancake breakfasts. Sue Halsey was waiting tables that morning and as she approached our table, she paused, took a closer look at Dick, and blurted out, "Hey! I know you!"

Dick smiled coyly and said, "From television?"

"No," Sue said, "You're the guy who was peeing up against the post office last night!"

All I could think was how foolish I'd been not to get photos for the *National Enquirer*.

20
The Simple Life

I loved teaching when my students were hippies. They would take a class, listen to a lecture, and read a textbook from front to back, simply because it was interesting. They didn't care about a bottom line, which, I suspect, is why so many of them are wealthy today. They knew that learning is its own reward and has nothing to do with money except that the more you know about anything, the more likely you are to make money doing anything else.

The one thing they did that vexed me, however, was that they would come to my office (they trusted me because I was a hippie too—still am) and announce that they were going off to Nevada to buy three acres of land, start an organic farm, live by their own labors, and enjoy—oh God!—the simple life! Although it never did any good until two years later when I could say "I told you so," at this point I would launch into an hours-long lecture about how we lead "the simple life" while so-called "primitive peoples," or our own pioneer peoples, led incredibly complex lives.

Sure, we have complicated technology around us—computers, televisions, thermostatically controlled heating and cooling systems, microwave ovens, unbelievably complicated automobiles, unconquerable lids on aspirin bottles—but our relationship with all that is simple to the point of being primal. What do you know about your microwave oven? On, off, set the timer. If you're like me, you don't even know how to do that preset timer thingie where it starts heating your breakfast oatmeal in the middle of the night. I consider myself to be something of a mechanic . . . but not on a modern automobile. I can't even find the carburetor on the damn thing. (There is no carburetor on the damn thing? Injectors? What's an injector? Where is the injector? You don't know either? Hmmm. . . .)

But pioneers, Australian aborigines, the Plains Pawnee, now there are complex lives. These people had to deliver their own children, forecast their own weather, provide their own entertainment, at least repair and probably manufacture their own tools. They not only had to cook their own food, but they had to find it. They had to be their own lawyers and doctors, know how to build an all-night fire, repair a kerosene lantern, chip a blade from stone, outwit each and every enemy—and some friends—and on and on and on. All of those dimensions of living that we currently hand over to others, they assigned to their own wit.

That was the good part. And that's what we miss. We are helpless in the face of all this complexity. No matter how good you are at doing your own plumbing, wiring, welding, or housebreaking of the dogs, there is inevitably something else you have to depend on someone else to do for you. No matter how many things you control, there are inevitably a universe of things you have absolutely no control over.

21

Take Control of Your Life—Yeah, Sure!

My theory is that that sense of helplessness generates a huge proportion of the mental anguish that is an intricate part of modern living. We don't know why the damn car broke down yesterday, or why the lights went off for three hours the day before, or why the goldfish all died on the same day last week, or why you have this constant pain in your butt, or why you simply cannot afford to buy cheese any more and yet the government is giving it away to some people. There isn't much we have control over, to be perfectly honest. That is to say, it's the simplicity of this arrangement that kills us.

So, what do we do to ease our troubled souls about this situation? We go camping, that's what. We leave perfectly good houses, with all those wonderful labor- and time-saving conveniences, and we go some place where we can start a fire and bat mosquitoes and catch fish for supper, no matter how messy it is or bad it tastes. When camping, we wind up pooping in outhouses and peeing up against a tree despite all that money we poured into perfectly good porcelain. But when we are camping, we have at least some modicum of that control we want, some feeling of that complexity that shows we can actually do some things for ourselves.

And I think that's one reason, probably a big reason, I love my outhouse.

We have three bathrooms in our big old farmhouse. The main one downstairs is constantly clogging—something about the septic tank, or drain field. The guy who comes out with the huge truck and pumps out all that crap once or twice a year says it may have something to do with antibiotics the ladies of the house take. I don't know.

The toilet in the bathroom upstairs is constantly running. It is an automatic response within our family now that as you pass by that bathroom, you step inside and jiggle the toilet handle. Sometimes it then stops running. On the other hand, sometimes it doesn't. You want to be real careful not to flush this toilet while the one downstairs is clogged, because then everything you are sending down the pipe winds up gushing into the downstairs toilet, over the bowl and out onto the floor. The faucet also drips and has built up an ugly deposit in the sink. Linda and Antonia hate it. When you turn off the faucet on the tub, the entire piping system throughout the house slams like a huge boiler exploding.

My own toilet in the back room keeps getting loose on its base. It clogs up now and then but not as bad as the one downstairs. Some kind of black slimy stuff insists on growing in the toilet reservoir. It may have something to do with the development of new biological sequences necessary to saving life on earth as we know it, but I still pour some Clorox in there now and then to kill it all off. God is going to have to find some place other than my bathroom toilet reservoir to start a new evolutionary chain.

Then there is my outhouse. Its mechanics are easily analyzed. Once every couple of years or so I may have to dig a new hole and move it, but on the other hand, it may be three or five years before I have to take care of that chore. Depends. (I don't know upon what that difference depends, however. I'd prefer not to know.) I can fix anything at all that goes wrong with my outhouse's system. I have replaced the hinges on the door, reroofed it, removed wasp nests, replaced the coffee can holding the toilet paper, and I put in the picture window myself.

I fix all the outhouse problems myself. My relationship with my outhouse is complicated. I am its constructor, its locator, its engineer, its operator, a full (as it were) partner in a mutual and extensive relationship. I serve it, it serves me.

My relationship with our indoor toilets is simple: Call the plumber.

22
Author's Afterword
to the Above Passage

In the first draft of this book I ended the chapter right there, at the period after "plumber." But I think I really need to clarify that statement. As it stands, it suggests that calling a plumber ends indoor toilet problems. This may not be the case, especially if the plumbers are anything like the plumbers where I live. I am thinking specifically of my buddy Woodrow, who is a plumber. He put the plumbing in our house. We bought an ancient, abandoned farmhouse, a really good deal for $350, a price that included a stained glass window and an etched window, some lovely woodwork, lots of stories and history. But we had to put a lot of time, money, and effort into totally rebuilding the interior, including the plumbing.

When the house was done and we moved in, it was a joyous moment. Linda stepped into her new, shiny kitchen and up to the splendid new double sink with gleaming faucets. She had always wanted a new, shiny kitchen. Then Antonia ran upstairs to the huge, ancient bath tub with the fancy antique handles and she turned on the water just for the joy of seeing that marvelous old giant in its functional glory. And the water went down the drain. And through the heating vents. And out the heating vent in the kitchen, right above the new sink.

I don't know a lot about plumbing but it has always struck me that the shiny copper tubes that characterize plumbing would be pretty hard to confuse with the big, boxy, galvanized ducts that seem fairly typical of heating systems. But somehow Woodrow had experienced that confusion, probably, I would guess, latish on a Friday afternoon or ear-lyish on a Monday morning. The heating ducts, not being installed with the idea of conducting water from the bathtub to the downstairs kitchen sink, leaked generously and to this day large, brown stains on our kitchen ceiling acknowledge Woodrow's error.

Woodrow was in our kitchen at the time this all happened, enjoying some celebratory beer on the occasion of us moving into a brand new house. Linda had a talk with him, a conversation not extending much beyond three or four words as I recall. He put down his half-empty beer, a gesture that is not at all typical of him, got a mess of tools from his truck, and within the hour he had reengineered the bathtub drain to conform to the more conventional model of emptying into the main drain pipe and out to our septic system.

All of which is to say, sometimes calling a plumber is not a final solution to your plumbing problems. Sometimes your wife needs to talk with the plumber.

23
The Society of Privacy

If you think about it, and I have, eating is a pretty disgusting process. You tear dead animals and plants into pieces suitable for stuffing into the wet maw of your carrier organism, grind it into a gooey mess, and mix it with various secretions that cause it to break down into its constituents. Next spasming throat muscles force this ground up paste into a larger container filled with acids and enzymes that further convert these animal and plant parts into even more disgusting substances. And yet, as repellent as eating is, it is one of our most basic social ways of establishing relationships—business, social, religious, family.

Elsewhere, notably in my book *Diggin' In and Piggin' Out*, I have theorized that the reasons we insist on sharing this basically obnoxious behavior with others are that (1) we want to demonstrate a primal willingness to overcome and set aside one of the most fundamental impulses of any animal, the impulse to survive by eating, and (2) to become vulnerable, to demonstrate trust to other organisms we want to like us or at least trust us, by letting them observe our fallibility. That is, we tell this potential business partner or bed partner across the table from us that, yeah, (1) they can have some of our food, and (2) sure, I'm a slob—just look at this huge stain I just made on my shirt—but I'm going to trust you enough to presume you are also going to share some food with me and that you're not going to point and laugh at the gravy on my shirt. And hey, maybe you'll buy some of these industrial-grade frimbles I'm trying to sell you. Or eventually go to bed with me and do things a lot more disgusting than eating.

But we humans aren't quite so sanguine about sharing our toilets. And I believe the same goes for animals, but more about that later. I have the distinct impression that the mere fact that there are conventionally two places to sit in an outhouse does not at all mean that it is often occupied by two people at the same time. Isn't that your impression too? I'll have more to say about that later too.

24
The Exposure of Indecency

Of course, the degree of one's willingness to share this end of the digestive system does vary from culture to culture to some degree. Do they still have *pissoirs* in Paris? It's been 45 years since I was there, but at that time the pissoir, a streetside urinal, was a standard feature of the Parisian scene and an object of amusement but certainly not disgust or contempt. The distinctive construction of a *pissoir* was that it had a screen that concealed the user only from the knees to the chest. Thus, a man could be standing there relieving himself while still exercising the courtesy of tipping his hat to ladies passing by. The pissoir seemed to me as a young American to admit to the obvious—that people pee—in contrast to the common and bizarre attitude of my American compatriots—that people do not. We would rather force people into peeing in alleys up against walls so we can arrest them for "indecent exposure." I can remember being stunned when I learned that "indecent exposure," along with the less benign meaning of exposing oneself to children, ladies, and undercover police officers (as so often seems to be the case) includes the inescapable pressures of needing to pee!

It was as much as anything those Parisian pissoirs that poked holes in my youthful belief that life in America is just about as close to perfect as life can be and that all other nations are barbaric in comparison. That and great bread. And good wine. And cheese.

Society and the Outhouse

One of my favorite writers, Wright Morris (I know, I said that before, but it's still true) captures for me the very essence of my attraction to the rural outhouse. Not only in terms of why an outhouse is better than an inhouse, but also why rural life is so damn much better for the soul than city life. Morris writes:

> When I was a boy, I did my thinking under the front porch, in the soft, hot dust, or on the small hole in Mr. T. B. Horde's three-seater privy. From the small hole I had a pretty good view of the town. I could watch the buggies come and go, and on a clear day I'd follow the trains, with their trail of smoke, across the valley to the west. I'd say this is the rural chapel, where a man puts his cares in order, or forgets his cares and turns his mind to other things. A good Sears & Roebuck watch, with a fob, or a pair of Monkey Ward green leather shoes. If the watch section happened to be gone, a man could reconsider bone-handled knives, ladies' corsets, or the shadowy teams of horses in their nickel-plated harness, pulling a tassel-fringed gig. Any boy who knew his catalogue—from abdominal belts to zinc—and had a three-seater privy along with it, would find the *Arabian Nights*, as I

found them, pretty dull stuff. What in Arabia could compare with a rubber-tired Irish Mail, a Ranger bike, or your initials on the back of a gold-looking stem-wind watch? Yours—carpet or no carpet—for handshelling 30 bushels of popcorn, or merely by subscribing half the people in the county to the *Saturday Evening Post.* But there were no Sears & Roebuck catalogues on 53rd Street (in the city). No privy, with a view of the valley, no unhinged door, no sun on your knees, no slow freights or fast grand-daddy longlegs, no buggies with the whip up, flowering, like a cow's tail, no prowling cats, or curious peering leghorns, no a-loneliness, nothing but the damned tiled privacy. Places to worry, that is, but no place to think. (Page 109)

There are a lot of things that recommend that paragraph to the serious outhouse reader. Like so much of Morris's writing (or any good writing), the more times you read it, the more reason you find to read it again. Isn't it interesting, for example, how he seems to think of privacy? In the city, it's "damned tiled privacy," but in the country it's almost a matter of public interaction. That's not just Wright Morris; that's all of us, I think.

26
Solo Performances

W̲e really do want privacy of some kind in our bathroom activities, but not necessarily the kind of privacy that springs first to mind. Notice, for example, that T. B. Horde's privy was a three-holer. Now, for those of you who have never experienced the pure joy of "the sun on your knees," the notion of a multiple-holed might seem curious if not downright disgusting. But such arrangements were not usually meant for multiple occupation; the various shapes and sizes of the holes were to accommodate the various shapes and sizes of visitors: a large ovalish hole for males, a smaller round one for ladies, and an even smaller round one for children, who seem always to harbor a primal, one might say with some poetic justice a deep-seated, fear of falling through privy holes into the nether world.

And yet this is an activity we all share as surely as we all breathe. Elimination is even more common, after all, than sex. There are people who go through life without experiencing the pleasures and discomforts of sex, even people who deliberately accept such deprivation as a personal commitment, but no one takes vows of eternal poverty, humility, and constipation. It just isn't done. So why are we embarrassed by something so totally expected of all of us?

That's not a rhetorical question because a rhetorical question presumes that the person who poses it has an answer. I don't have an answer. In fact, I have even more questions.

Outhouses

Thirty years ago I was a faculty member in a wonderful education experiment known as Centennial Education at the University of Nebraska. I have often heard from former students that this free and open approach to learning changed their minds and souls, but the fact of the matter is it also profoundly affected the way many of us on the faculty went about teaching, learning, and thinking too. I won't go into exactly how that program worked. This isn't the place for it, and of course it has since died, the University of Nebraska wanting to dedicate even more of its energies, monies, and resources to football for the few, rather than education for the many.

But here's what I'm getting at: Centennial was a residential program. We occupied a large, older building that had previously been a women's dorm. All the students lived in that building, we faculty had our offices there, and rooms scattered around the structure served as classrooms, insofar as we used classrooms at all. It was a coed program, wonderfully free in a hippie world, and there simply never were better students than hippies. They saw learning as a joyful process in its own, without any reference whatsoever to a "bottom line."

Up to the time I became a fellow, which is what we called faculty members at Centennial, I had been a conventional teacher, conventional and boring as hell (although not as boring as my even duller colleagues, which is why I was tapped for Centennial). But more than that, I had also been a pretty conventional, Nebraska, middle-income, plain-thinking, standard, run-of-the-mill nonrevolutionary sort of guy. And one of the most startling things I ran into as I started my first weeks at Centennial was something that was never discussed, explained, excused, or apparently so much as noticed by anyone—student or faculty. There was a toilet on each floor of the building and that toilet was also coed.

To this day boneheaded prigs, lawmakers, officials, functionaries, and bureaucrats in Nebraska—and I suspect everywhere else—fret and stew about sexual equality: "My god! Next thing you know, they're going to want to be using the same bathrooms!" Never mind that we all do use the same bathrooms in airplanes, or for that matter, our homes. That is serial unisex elimination. Centennial was a community of a couple hundred people, with two or three bathrooms, so there was indeed coincidental stool occupation from time to time.

27
Multigender Visits

I discovered the coed nature of our bathrooms when I was relieving myself and a young lady came in and occupied the stool next to me. I think that this arrangement was never mentioned to me as a deliberate gesture of contempt toward anyone who thought such a thing needed mentioning. The only time, in fact, that anyone brought up this unusual arrangement was an occasion when some of the particularly retarded members of our state legislature were making a major fuss about this kind of potential horror. It may have been in connection with a debate concerning women serving in the military and the certain total disaster that would occur if men and women actually had to use the same slit trench. We Centennial people chuckled rather quietly up our sleeves, wondering what those very same solons would think if they knew that at that very moment they were funding an educational program at their very own land-grant college, where young men and women peed together and where the faculty and students openly admitted that both sexes poop!

We still wrestle with this incredible idiocy, much more freely accepted in Europe, where coed bathrooms, while not inevitable, are at least more common. An article in our newspaper lamenting the demise of the television series *Ally McBeal* comments that one of the most controversial and daring features of that show, where various couples freely coupled in all manner of combinations—apparently the

characters were completely at the command of their hor-
mones, lusting like slavering animals, humping couch legs,
and having accidents in their pants at the mere passing of an
attractive potential bed partner—is a unisex bathroom, à la
Centennial Education. I don't know what Americans think
will happen if men and women use the same bathroom . . .
probably an Ally McBeal thing, where the mere sound of a
gorgeous woman farting sends a happily married man into
paroxysms of lust and gays run amok at the mere hint of body
functions. But it is my impression that one of the least sexy
things we do is use a toilet. Of course since the same thing
could be said of eating, uh, well, there you are.

I will address the toilet as a communications terminal
later, but I think I should mention at this point that the
stalls at Centennial also served that function. Human beings
have almost forever considered a toilet a place to express
themselves by writing on the walls. An interesting feature of
Centennial and other unisex toilets however is that while it
can be presumed by men using men's rooms that the readers of their wall scrawlings will be other men, in a coed toilet the assumption has to be otherwise. At least some readers will be the opposite sex. Curiously, in my opinion at
least, this realization mellowed and almost romanticized the
traditionally crude nature of bathroom wall writing. In
other words, precisely as we expect with governmental
thinking, the reality is almost exactly the opposite of official
expectations.

Modesty is a very peculiar emotion. We tend to think of
it as being natural. Of course a woman doesn't want to show
off her boobs. They are ferociously sexual objects, after all,
and if she were to walk around with her boobs hanging out,
men would go bonkers and God only knows what would
happen next. Right? But of course women do want to show
off their boobs. And men like that and can enjoy it without
turning into ballroom floor rapists. And there are societies
in the world where women's breasts are routinely bare, and

men actually interact with bare-breasted women without staggering around, struggling to compensate for eternal erections.

Moreover, in some societies, what a woman normally exposes in our society—her mouth, her ankles, a knee—is considered impossibly immoderate and arousing. The fact of the matter is, what we feel comfortable exposing or viewing, what is arousing and what is disgusting, what is moral and what is immoral is largely arbitrary. That is, as a culture, over time and by tradition, we decide what is immodest, and then that becomes for us what is indeed immodest.

And even that has a latitude far wider than we might expect.

I used to teach summer courses in literature and culture here on my farm when there was nothing more by way of buildings than a single-room log house and a privy. A class of maybe 20 students would gather here for a week or two, and we studied plains literature, history, folklore, and culture. It was a great place to study such things, an isolated, pioneer log house, deep in a woods along a river bottom, right out in nature, where the literature, culture, folklore, and history actually happened . . . and happens. We cooked pioneer and Indian foods, and even when the day's lectures and discussions ended, we continued our conversations about the one thing we had in common—our studies—well into the night.

Some of the older and local students simply drove to their homes when the day ended, and that was fine. The rest of us, perhaps a dozen or so, stayed at the cabin. Now, I can imagine some eyebrows already raising at this situation. Hmmm . . . men and women sleeping in the same room, well, I see. Hmmm . . . Before you get too outraged, it's going to get worse. These classes of mine were in June and July. In Nebraska. It was hot and dirty. We cooked over an open fire, in the wind and dust of the Great Plains, in the sun, and the only facilities I had for bathing was the river, a wonderfully clean, placid, sandy flow of water.

Roger Welsch

I made this situation clear, and said that I was headed down to the river to wash up, that anyone who cared to come along was welcome, anyone who wanted to go separately at another time could, blah, blah, blah, trying to accommodate any of the various possible personal levels of modesty within the group. And then I'd grab a bar of soap and a towel and head off for the river.

I suppose it was then a matter of peer pressure, not wanting to seem chicken, but it was also and perhaps even more clearly a matter of wanting to be clean and comfortable. Moreover, I have found (as in the case of Centennial's unisex bathrooms) a great and immediate flexibility in most people in adjusting to such situations: When it doesn't seem to make any difference, well, it just doesn't seem to make any difference. Whatever the case, almost inevitably everyone in the party grabbed their towels and soap bars and traipsed along through the woods behind me. At the river, we shed our clothes, more often than not continuing marvelously civilized discussions of literary motifs, historical processes, and cultural conflicts, and waded out into the cool, clean water naked as jaybirds.

In the years I did that, there was never a single incidence of discomfort or embarrassment, much less assault or insult. A set of rules seemed automatically to spring full grown, as if, well, natural. No staring. No comments. And nothing implied. That is, although we may have bathed together totally naked the third week in June, when we were back on campus in September, it was Professor Welsch this, and Miss Hotovy that. No prurient conclusions were drawn. In fact—I'm not kidding—it was almost as if we respected each other more clothed because we had respected each other naked. Because we had exposed such incredible intimacy, and therefore vulnerability, we had all the more reason to demonstrate our civility and propriety in other circumstances. Curiously, my own experiences suggest that things like unisex bathrooms might lead to more civility and courtesy, rather than less.

Wow.

28
The Uninvited Intruders

One incident in particular underscored this notion of mine about modesty even more. My class and I were walking along a beautiful white sand shore, headed upstream to a deeper channel. Remember, we are all stark naked. And we were, no kidding, talking about some feature of plains culture and literature, maybe something about the nature of plains rivers being aggrading rather than erosive, the sands of the Sandhills, the riparian forest, whatever. We got to the river bank and were about to pass around the clump of willows and enter the wonderfully refreshing water when, to our utter surprise, two canoes came around the corner, not 20 feet from us.

Our screaming was deafening; our scramble for cover chaotic. The people in the canoes paddled furiously and turned away from us. We dove behind trees and turned our backs. In a few seconds the canoes were again out of sight. We emerged from our cover, giggling uncomfortably, blushing, abashed, and went back to our business . . . of being naked together again.

Now, wouldn't logic suggest that we should be embarrassed about being naked with classmates and a faculty member, people we would see the next morning at breakfast, people we would see again formally on a campus, much more than four strangers we'd never see again? I sure would think so. But that is not at all the way it went on that occasion.

Roger Welsch

Thing is, we had established those tacit understandings I list-
ed above. We had an agreement about mutual acceptance,
self-control, civility, courtesy, respect. But we had no such
agreement with these strangers in the canoes. They weren't in
on this silent détente about not noticing, much less com-
menting on boobs or wienies or asses, the abundance or lack
of same, the peculiarities or magnificence of them, the mere
fact that, well, and in some cases, wow, there they were.

29
The Privacy of the Privy

Our social contract regarding bathroom privacy is, I guess, much the same as the social contract regarding nudity. It's surprise that disconcerts. What is agreed on, even without a word spoken, is acceptable to a degree we simply cannot predict or expect in advance. Do I have a story to illustrate this? Hey, you know me. Of course I have a story to illustrate this! Our home is a huge, old farmhouse we moved into and rebuilt. We were in the middle of that process 20 years ago when two former students dropped in. They had been here before, probably for one of my summer workshops, and since they were in the neighborhood, they thought they'd stop by. They were surprised to find that in addition to the simple log house down by the river, there was now this big, old, shaggy farmhouse in the process of being refurbished.

The students looked the situation over and announced that they were making their way around the countryside earning money for school the next fall by painting houses. They had a truckload of equipment and, saying they had appreciated my class and felt they might just owe me a little something, offered to paint the house, no small offer since this is a huge old house, two stories high on the north side, three on the south. Of course I jumped at their offer, tossing in a promise of food and beer for the duration of their stay.

They hauled out their equipment and proceeded to paint that house—and my outhouse—and for a couple evenings we also had some good times discussing our previous encounters. They finished their work and began the long, messy job of cleaning off all their equipment. We worked at the job through the morning and at some point, I detected the distinctive throb of a helicopter approaching, low, and guessed out loud that the medical evacuation team must be passing through, maybe hauling someone to the hospital in Grand Island, or on a training exercise up toward St. Paul, our county seat.

Sure enough, moments later the helicopter with its big red crosses on its sides and bottom came zooming over the river and straight toward and over our house. But it just whizzed over the house when it wheeled suddenly, went back south, turned and headed north toward us again. I commented on this strange maneuver to the student who was standing there with me cleaning painting equipment.

The chopper came back over us, even lower, and now we could see the passengers in the plane looking down at us from the front bubble. Hmmm. "What do you suppose that is about?" my friend asked. I guessed that maybe they often flew this route but had never seen this splendid, newly painted white house glowing in Nebraska's summer sun before. They flew over us, same path, again, and wheeled again as they passed over the house, repeating the loop, circling back and once again passing, still lower, directly over the house. This time we could see the pilots and medical personnel pointing at us and laughing.

Hmmm . . . What could that possibly be about?

At that very moment the other student exited the outhouse 30 feet from us and facing the river—the direction from which the chopper had made its three passes over us—pulling up his pants and muttering, "You'd think they'd never seen a guy with his overalls down around his ankles before." Here were doctors and nurses, medical pilots, people who had seen their share of people, bare knees, poopers, chamber pots, bed pans, whatever, but this time they had happened on someone who was (1) helpless and (2) not in on the "agreement." And they had taken full advantage of their good luck. It wasn't so much his quasi-nudity. However boastful he might be, please, how much could they see from 500 feet in the air and traveling at 150 miles per hour? It was his surprise and discomfort that gave them such glee. And to this day gives me glee in the retelling.

In a social situation men may be less modest about discussing the demands of their bladders, using pseudo-euphemisms like "shake the dew off the lily," "shake hands with the unemployed," and "see a man about a horse," but we all demonstrate a kind of uneasiness about admitting that we do what everyone does. We never blurt out unabashedly where exactly we are heading and what exactly we intend to do there unless we are with a bunch of buddies and have been drinking beer for a couple hours, in which case men usually feel free to say something like, "Jeez, but if I don't pee right now, I'm going to explode!"

Anyone who is not familiar with how the outhouse concept, especially in a nonrural situation such as a small town or village might wonder how one avoided or (in some few oh-so-fortunate situations) still avoids the embarrassment of being seen by all the world traipsing out to the privy to, well, you know. In days past some artifices were used to buffer the blunt truth of what was about to happen at the end of that long, sometimes hurried, all-too-public walk to the "back house." For example, a woodpile was often placed near the outhouse or between the main house and the outhouse, I am told, so that one could look on at least part of the trip as if it were not necessitated by bodily functions, but rather its purpose was to collect fuel for the family hearth. My own inclination, having both relied on wood heat and an outhouse, is the opposite: one always multitasks in such situations, bringing in wood, hauling out ashes, checking the horses, and carrying out the garbage all in the same trip, no matter what intestinal process originally necessitated the venture into the cold.

30
The Small Town's System

I have lived a good deal of my life in association with a small town. While small communities do indeed tend to be socially conservative—almost islands of Victorian prudery—the residents of such communities seem less inhibited about admitting that there are bodily functions associated with things like outhouses. The thing is, in such settings one is expected simply to make more of an effort at not noticing them. Or maybe, in noticing them, not make much of them. Everyone in a small town knows everything. But you don't have to make a big production out of what you know—especially if you are going to face the very same kind of public witness before long yourself.

Twenty-five years ago I came here to my own small community (population 352) from a very urban setting, so the differences in such lifestyles are particularly vivid to me. I am a liberally inclined, educated, unpretentious, even audacious kind of a guy. But even I was surprised when I encountered uneasy, almost secretive reluctance if I might suggest that some buddies and I go over to Dick's place and borrow his table saw or ask him if he wanted to go fishing:

Me: "Let's run over to Dick's and check with him."

Buddies: "Uh, maybe we should check with Chuck instead".

Me: "But I know Dick is home today and." . . .

Buddies: "Let's go check with Chuck."

Outhouses

Buddies [with visible discomfort]: "Well, you know, uh, today is Thursday. And Thursday afternoon is, well, er, Dick and Betty's, uh, 'special time,' if you catch my drift."

Gradually I figured out that you don't bother Bob and Liz on Friday mornings, Chris and Heather on Saturday mornings, or Al and Bernice damn near any noon of the week. I suppose that could be seen as an indictment of small-town life, a matter of prying, of knowing too much, but in a way it is also a convenience, going about one's, uh, business knowing that you probably won't be interrupted. After all, everyone knows it's, er, your special time. The point, it seems to me, is not to deny what we all do but to be discreet enough to respect the privacy of those activities. So everyone in a small town not only knew that you were headed out to the outhouse, and could tell by the length of your visit what your particular activity might be while there, they would also probably note that you were a quarter-hour earlier than usual and spent an extra 10 minutes out there. "Saw Emmy cutting cabbage out in the yard all morning so I suspect that that special coleslaw recipe of hers has activated old Elmer's innards again, don't you expect? Happens every time."

The point is not to pretend those things don't happen but to respect your neighbors' privacy and not to make a fuss about them, although a friendly mention at choir practice the next night that a good helping of cottage cheese often helps with such distress might be appropriate.

31

Does a Polar Bear Poop on the Ice?

Next time you are sitting in your outhouse daydreaming, try to conjure up the most wonderful fantasy you can. Go wild. No limits. Riches, sex, travel, power. For years I did that, but my wildest dream came true. No, not the one with Cindy Crawford, Claudia Schiffer, and Heather Locklear on the round bed with satin sheets in the room dimly lit with sandalwood candles. As if I would have degenerate notions like that. . . . No, I'm thinking of the fantasy I had since I was 14 or 15 and had the Norwegian friend who wound up in the U.S. Air Force stationed at Thule, Greenland. Jeez, I remember drooling even then and writing him questions about that starkly beautiful place. Had he actually seen that three-mile-thick ice sheet covering the naked rock? (It is almost within walking distance of the base, he told me.) Had he met Inuits? (Many work at the base, and the village of Qaanaaq, the northernmost human habitation on earth, is a bit over an hour's flight to the north.) Is the weather as brutal as rumored? (Every room on the base has a supply of food. During Class III storms, you may not leave your room, much less your building, even to save a stranded colleague, because mere moments in that severe environment will kill you.)

Thing is, I love winter. My favorite movie is the Robert Altman film *Quintet* with Paul Newman. You've never seen it. No one has. I have a copy, and when I share it with friends they think I'm nuts, because its visions of an ice sheet—the very ice sheet my Norwegian friend had seen!—covering North America are so brutal that the film is crushing. To everyone, that is, but me. My heart beats in sympathy with Essex Redstone when he turns his back on the degeneracy of the city and trudges back out onto the purity of the ice. I don't know how often I have waded through the snow to my own town, stumbling into the steamy, dark tavern with icicles hanging from my mustache, imagining myself to be Essex Redstone, coming in to see if mankind is yet showing any signs of redemption. (It never is. Certainly not in the Dannebrog tavern!)

My dream for 50 years was to go to Thule. But of course that would never happen. There is only one weekly flight to Thule, and if there is bad weather, not even that. The plane that makes that weekly hop is called the "DC-late." It flies out of Baltimore and has about 10 seats for personnel, while the rest of the huge plane is jammed full of supplies and equipment. Ships can reach the outpost only during the few days when the bay ice thaws in August. But my dreams would not go away. Not for 50 years.

I got a piece of fan mail a couple years ago from a reader named Dean Vinson, thanking me because my humorous treatment of the hobby of restoring old tractors had convinced his girlfriend that he was indeed marriageable and she had accepted his proposal on the basis of my insistence that the activity is harmless. Nice note. I was pleased. I wrote back to him, just as I respond to all such nice letters. But then I noticed, oh my God! His e-mail address said . . . *Thule!* Ultima Thule, the most northward. Within snowball-throwing distance of the North Pole!

I wrote to Dean and told him about my dream. And I asked if there was any way he could get me up there? To entertain the troops (I make my living as a banquet speaker)? As a teacher (I taught at the university level most of my life)? As a television personality (I was an essayist for CBS News *Sunday*

Morning at the time)? As a stowaway? He asked in return how much it would cost for me to come to entertain at the base service club. I said that if he could get me within a mile of the base, I would swim the rest of the way. He said there'd be no swimming. The ice is 12 feet thick on the sea most of the time.

The bottom line is that he got me to Thule. It was one of those rare events in my life—probably anyone's life—when the realization of a dream is every bit as wonderful as the fantasy. Even better. The Arctic is even more wonderful than I had imagined. I loved every instant of it. And one of the best parts was that I got to helicopter even farther north to Qaanaaq, an Inuit fishing and seal-hunting village. That alone was one of the most wonderful experiences of my life, but things just kept getting better. As we landed in Qaanaaq, the pilot turned to me and said, "You know, I have to make a quick run another hundred or so miles north to a little village called Sioropoluk, about 60 seal hunters up there. Wanna go?"

My god! I thought Qaanaaq was the northernmost human habitation on earth, and now I find there is something even farther north! I simply could not believe my good fortune, and of course I went. I never got to the village because we only paused at the pad while the Inuit Eskimos unloaded the cargo and passengers for that site—you don't turn off your engines and let them get cold when you are within walking distance of the North Pole!—but while we waited the pilot told me, "Step over there, to the north side of the helipad, beyond the guys unloading the stuff. Then you will be further north than only a handful of other people on earth." I did it and almost cried at the joy it gave me.

32
So, What *Do* Eskimos Do?

Then we returned to Qaanaaq, which seemed almost tropi-
cal in comparison, and spent some time there, looking out
over the frozen bay, eating seal, whale, walrus, and dried fish,
marveling at the geographic adaptability of man. And contemplating how we humans do what we need to do.

I won't ask you to try to imagine what life is like in
Qaanaaq. It's not something easily imagined. Most of the people in Qaanaaq—about 400 or 500 of them—have never seen
a tree except on videotapes, or seen edible plants growing. It's
rock and ice, and that's pretty much it. The Inuit stomach
flora is different from, say, a small-town Nebraska boy's. They
eat fish and fat; I would be sick as a dog on a diet like that.

For the Inuit, it is a fine place to live, no problems. Men
working around town wore T-shirts even though the temper-
ature never rose above freezing, rarely, in fact, rose above zero
Fahrenheit. (I was there in April.) But there are some accom-
modations involving more than physical adaptation. While
looking out over the frozen bay one day I noticed a front-end
loader and a large truck going out onto the sea ice and
approaching one of the many icebergs frozen into the sea ice.
Glacial ice is a spectacularly beautiful light blue. It is geologic
ice, frozen hundreds, sometimes thousands of years ago,
moving slowly down to the sea. It breaks loose from the front
of the glacier during the few days of summer when there is a
thaw and moves out the inlet, where it remains frozen in place
for almost a year until the next thaw.

Roger Welsch

The loader approached one of the stranded icebergs and began knocking loose large lumps and loading them into the truck. What was that all about? Our host at the Qaanaaq hotel explained that the icebergs are the village's source of fresh water. ("Hotel" may seem a bit unlikely a label, but while the hotel is Spartan, all life in Qaanaaq is Spartan, and the hotel and its few tiny rooms are really quite comfortable.) The man in the loader was bringing the hunks of ice back to the shore, selling them to village folks who put them on the front or back porches of their homes, breaking off chunks as they needed them. It is the finest fresh water you will ever drink, purer than any other water on earth. Even better, it sizzles when you drop a hunk into a glass of good bourbon! The point slowly soaked in, however, that the guy in the loader was making a living selling ice to Eskimos. You gotta love life when ironies like that appear so generously.

But that is not the thrust of this collection of essays. What of the other dimensions of the biology here? Well, as is so often the case, that is quite another issue. Outside all those colorful, small houses in Qaanaaq, the ones with the hunks of pure blue glacial ice on the porch, there are also huge hunks of gray ice. All the toilets in Qaanaaq are chemical and a utilities truck comes around regularly to empty them. I don't know and don't want to know what they do with the ugly-buglies from that operation. But what happens with all that gray water is less subtle.

See, they can't run sewers down to the sea or to a processing plant. This "gray water" from bathing, dish washing, face washing, and tooth brushing would freeze up instantly. It wouldn't help to put the lines under the ground. The ground (such as it is—it is mostly rock) is eternally frozen solid too. So, waste water dribbles out of each house and builds up over the winter into a huge gray ice mound. The size of these waste water mountains is at least restricted in part because water is in short supply too; even seawater freezes, after all. In Qaanaaq, Greenland, everything freezes.

33
Come the Thaw

Until spring. Or rather, summer. Things thaw out for only a couple months a year and that is the summer. And then it really thaws because just as the sun never appears in the winter, in the summer it never goes down. I was there in April and could assure my wife Linda by telephone that I was in bed every night "before sundown," since the sun dipped below the horizon for only a few hours each night, even at that early time of the summer. And just as the problem during the frozen months is that there is no flowing water, the reverse is true during the thaw when everything turns to water. The ice on the mountains behind the town, the gray ice in the town, the sea ice, everything melts. And then floods rage through the town, turning it into a churning, stinky swamp. But these floods also mercifully sweep the whole mess down to the sea, where everything is washed even further out to sea, to be replaced by fresh icebergs and eventually fresh sea ice. Yeah, I suppose it's pollution, but with so few people so far away from everything and absolutely no alternative, it's pretty hard to get very excited about it.

If chemical toilets take care of human wastes in Qaanaaq, I then wondered about animal wastes. Dogs are essential to almost all activities in the Arctic. They are not pets, they are tools. And not just for hunters and fishermen. I treasure an image of a Qaanaaq shopper heading home with a wheelbar-row of supplies pulled by a dog in harness. So what happens to all that dog poop? We have three black labs and keeping up with those bozos' waste is quite enough of a job. What happens when you have a couple dozen sled dogs and no natural deterioration—everything is in a permanent deep freeze—or rain to wash it away like we have occasionally in Nebraska?

Well, for one thing, most of the dogs are kept out on the sea ice. And they are chained up. All dogs off chains are shot immediately in Qaanaaq. These dogs are mostly wolf and have the nasty habit of eating children, especially if they should happen to fall down on their way to school. On one hand, this means the frozen dog poop piles up, but it also means that the dogs can easily be relocated to a poop-free zone when necessary. And then when the sea ice melts, the dog poop goes away.

34
An Ancient Problem

The problem of waste disposal in a basic society is worth considering. (I prefer "basic" to "primitive," since I consider Inuit society far superior in almost all ways to our own.) I think poop is ignored far too often in anthropological situations. Just a few miles from where I sit on my Nebraska tree farm, there are signs of a pre-Pawnee village—pot shards, flint chips, bone fragments. It was occupied off and on for as much as a thousand years. But not continuously. A natural question would be, why not continuously? It is an almost idyllic site—excellent water, natural protection, rich soils, climactically sheltered. One could argue that over a relatively short period of time, wood resources would be exhausted, but a perfectly acceptable form of fuel was constantly being renewed all around them: buffalo chips. (Not at all as offensive as you might imagine, by the way.) Or that pressure from a belligerent neighbor forced a weaker population to move, but then there were always belligerent neighbors, as you probably already know if you live in a small town.

But human waste is not so generous in its advantages. Imagine if you can, and as briefly as you care, that you live in a small community of maybe 40 to 60 kinsman, young and old. And every day each of you poops. Probably a fairly short distance from where you cook, sleep, eat, and play. Even if the young have the strength to walk a distance to relieve themselves, the bowels have a way of making their requirements known, if you catch my drift. And the old and young may have the time, but they may not have the strength to walk a discreet mile or so from the village limits. I can imagine very easily that within a couple years at the long edge there would be more than enough reason for the good folks of your group to pack up their few belongings and move along to another site, even one less attractively situated, just to give the land and air a chance to flush.

Things must have been particularly critical, if you know what I mean, after a long winter on the plains when nobody wanted to travel very far from home through the bitter cold to take care of their daily pressures. There certainly weren't incentives for the villagers to practice such courtesies as digging holes in the rock-hard frozen ground and then covering up those holes before sauntering back through a driving blizzard and subzero temperatures to the warmth of a buffalo robe bed and the lodge fire! Nope, I suspect that you went just as far as you had to go, did what you had to do and nothing more than that, then headed back home.

And then came springtime. While the spring thaw and resultant floods are an inconvenience, at a minimum, to the Inuit of Qaanaaq, if there wasn't at least one spring gully-washer in a North American Indian village, well, you didn't go out with shovels and clean up a winter's worth of problems. It just thawed out and brought back to the nearby village memories of a whole winter's worth of short hikes that should have ideally been much longer.

And the consensus probably developed quickly: time for the village to move on.

Now, imagine larger settlements, like those of Mesa Verde, or the substantial Pawnee villages along the Nebraska Loup River complex. That's a lot of people, a lot of poop. Any more questions of why folks eventually decided it might be a good idea to move along to another base of operations for a while? Yikes.

Ponder all this the next time you turn up your nose about how primitive my outhouse is.

35
Speaking of Dogs

The dogs of Qaanaaq are beautiful creatures. But then I love dogs, so all dogs are beautiful to me. But the dogs of Qaanaaq are also hard-working beasts, and just inches away from their wolf ancestors. Which means they can be dangerous. Tourists are welcomed to Qaanaaq—there aren't many because it sure as hell isn't easy to get to Qaanaaq—but they are also warned to stay away from the dogs. One false move, one mistake, one errant odor, and you are playing with a pack of snarling carnivores.

They are perhaps the hardiest dogs in the world, just as their masters are some of the hardiest humans on earth. When they have shelters, they are actually igloos, cut out of the snow, or bare wind shelters not nearly as substantial as doghouses I see every day around my farm in central Nebraska. Most of the time, Eskimo dogs simply curl up in a tight furry bundle, squint their eyes against the blowing ice crystals, and go to sleep just as surely as if they were black labs basking in a May sun.

There is a law in Greenland, which is free-governed but still a part of Denmark, that no dogs other than Inuit sled dogs are allowed north of the Arctic Circle. They don't want to dilute that wonderful blood developed to such a fine edge over so many centuries, maybe millennia. So how does a little village in total isolation avoid a complete clogging up of the gene pool? The Eskimos notoriously practiced the gracious hospitality of offering the rare cross-icecap guest the use of one's wife during his stay, thus providing at least a chance of enriching the gene inventory, and much the same is done with dogs. A sled dog bitch in heat is sometimes staked well beyond the village limits, but within range of visiting wolves. And thus new genes are introduced to the pack. If a polar bear doesn't come along first and enjoy the chained dog in quite a less pleasant way.

I had some opportunities to watch sled dogs in action during my visit to the Far North. Not enough, however. They are marvelous beasts. If you don't know the North, or dogs, you might imagine that using dogs to haul heavy sledges with passengers, equipment, or carcasses from the hunt is a cruel burden for the canines. Ask a black Lab how much he hates going duck hunting! I have seen trucks around this town driving around for days with the back end full of black dogs with their tongues hanging out a foot, flicking spit for all the world like lawn sprinklers. No, they weren't hot, they were excited. Somewhere off in the distance they had heard a gun go off and in their passion to be there when the birds fall into the freezing water, they tore loose from their pens, yards, or leashes and ensconced themselves in the back of that truck, not to be dislodged for all the world's efforts until their master had the good sense to grab his shotgun too and head for the duck blind. It's easier just to leave those dogs in the back of the pickup truck for a couple days and drive them around town on various errands than to try to drag the brutes one by one out of the truck and back to the kennel.

Well, that's the way it is with sled dogs too. You don't have to ask them twice if they want to hook up to a sled and take off across the sea ice for 10 days of sleeping on the ice, eating dried fish, reeking of seal guts and blood, hauling a half-ton of dead meat 30 miles across razor-sharp ice. Ask any sled dog. He'll say, "*Yea! That's my favorite thing!*" So, sled dog drivers, or mushers as they are called, carry whips. But not to make the dogs go. The whip is used to make them stop.

Outhouses

I did not have the good fortune to go out on the sea ice with a dog sled, but my buddy Ed Brimner did. A friend of his asked him during our stay in Qaanaaq if he'd like to go on a sled ride out onto the sea ice. Of course he would. So they set off about 9 or 10 that evening, across the naked ice, between the icebergs, on a pleasant evening's jaunt. (Since it doesn't really get dark, it doesn't much matter what time of the day you set off on such larks.)

As I understand it, in Alaska and the Canadian north, sled dogs are rigged in a long line between two traces, like horses pulling a stagecoach. But the Greenlandic sea ice has cracks, gaps, and ridges that would make it very hard for dogs to work in the kind of unison required by a hitch like that. They need independence of action and movement to let them pull or not pull, jump, or pause as their situation demands. So in Greenland, the dogs are arranged in a fan, with a separate line running back from each dog to the sled. When Ed and his friend had traveled an hour or so out from the village, they had to stop to untangle all the lines. You can imagine all those wacky dogs going absolutely nuts with joy about being able to run insanely in accordance with everything in their breeding for the preceding 1,000 years or so. They crossed and criss-crossed and eventually wound up in a terrible tangle.

The woman driving the sled pulled it to a stop while she untangled the lines and let the dogs rest, although that was the last thing they had in mind. She had to crack her whip on occasion to keep the dogs crouching and cowering because the only thing on their minds was to continue the mad dash across the ice. I mean jeez, you know dogs!

Once the lines were untangled, Ed got back on the sled and huddled down in the furs and blankets. His friend got ready to go, put away her whip, and then initiated the elaborate, well timed choreography of giving the dogs the word to go, letting them get the sled started, and then leaping to her position on the sled, standing on the back of the runners and holding onto the vertical rear posts of the sled. All well and good when the process goes right. But on this occasion the woman said the magic word, the dogs leaped to full speed instantly, she jumped . . . and missed the runners.

Later that night—much later—Ed told me that after a few moments he realized he was alone, lying there on a sled, without a driver, careening insanely across the Arctic sea ice. He moved further and further away from the driver, further and further away from the faint traces of civilization that Qaanaaq represented out here in Nowhere. Ed is a very savvy guy, and cool, so he didn't panic. He had noticed that there is a kind of brake on the sleds, a short length of very large hawser rope, tied on the ends to longer, much lighter lines. The heavy rope is thrown forward under the runners of the sled and the severely increased drag brings the dogs to a stop. Eventually. So he threw the rope forward as best he could from his horizontal position, but the heavy rope fell under only one of the runners.

Which was not enough to slow the dogs, much less stop them. To add to the drag, Ed therefore leaned heavily over on the runner side with the rope under it. The sled hit a bump. And Ed was thrown out of the sled. Which the dogs, now utterly unencumbered, were carrying at full speed across the ice. Ed watched the dogs disappear into the distance, and turned to walk back to the sled's owner walking toward him from a mile or so behind. When they met, the woman said there was no sense in following the dogs: They would eventually wind up at the head of the fjord, hopelessly tangled in their lines, and furious with frustration tear each other apart. There was nothing to do but walk the long miles back to the village across the ice.

But they had only walked back perhaps a mile or two when they heard a sound behind them, back in the direction the dogs had disappeared, and here they came back, still running full speed, right straight at them. The woman stood her ground in front of them as they came howling up and dragged them to a stop by grabbing the lines. She said the

Outhouses

dogs had almost certainly been spotted by some seal hunters out on the ice and they knew immediately what had happened. The sled was a runaway and that meant that somewhere someone was stranded out on the cold, dangerous sea ice. But these people, who had worked all their lives with dogs, also knew that if you turn sled dogs around in their own tracks, they will follow those tracks right back the direction from which they came. Which they did.

36
Dogs Farther South

Like I said, remarkable beasts, those sled dogs! But they are still dogs. Which is to say, they are embarrassed when they poop. I don't understand that at all. Dogs love to watch each other pee. And you know the kind of fascination they have in other dogs' butts. But most dogs are genuinely embarrassed when they poop. We just got a new puppy, Allie McBeelzebub, and I watched her with scientific interest to see at what point a dog develops this self-awareness. She is three-quarters black Lab, one quarter St. Bernard, the latter being unfortunately the quarter that eats and poops. From her very first evacuations in our yard she was embarrassed, sought out privacy, looked nervously over her shoulder, and walked away from her Big Stinkies with a clear air of "Who, me? I didn't do anything. I have no idea who made that mess back there!"

The next time you're driving along or walking along somewhere and you see a dog pooping, looking frantically in all directions, teetering dangerously on way too narrow a wheel base, shivering, ears down almost to his elbows, yell something derisive. Make some kind of smart remark: "Hey, mutt! Been eating cheese?" "Fido, don't forget to kick a little loose grass over that!" "Genius! You got some on your tail!" And you will see one humiliated dog.

I don't do such things, because I feel sorry for the dog thus caught in midevacuation and am therefore protective of his or her dignity. My good ol' Lab Lucky, may he rest in

Outhouses

peace, would start a major pooping project and happen to spot me sitting on the porch swing. He would pinch that thing off in midpressure and remove his activities to the north side of the house just to avoid the embarrassment. Imagine the city dog who has to do his duty with all manner of witnesses and then look on as his "master" scoops the still-steaming mess into a plastic bag to take home as if it were leftovers. I can't imagine.

37
And Then There's Cats

Cats are not like that. They feign modesty but they will rattle, scratch, bang, and shuffle for a quarter-hour in a kitty litter box just to make damn sure someone catches their act and appreciates their delicacy and gentility.

Cats don't fool me. Cats do fool a lot of people. I once had a cat named Judy who hated me because he was a male. It was my mistake, of course, I apologized for this gaffe of nomenclature but Judy took it very personally, apparently. I had a fireplace in my office and loved to build a nice warm blaze on a winter day when I was trying to get the Muse to notice me and kiss my brow. But then I began to notice that when I built a fire on a previous blaze's ashes, the room was filled not with the satisfying perfume of a good, clean, hardwood fire but with a pungent, not at all pleasant stink, something like burning cat poop. Mostly because it was burning cat poop.

One day while I was working away, trying to write something that would make some money to pay the rent for Judy's shelter, buy the fuel for Judy's comfort, and purchase the food for Judy's refined tastes, Judy walked into my study. He stopped and looked at me long enough to make sure I stopped my typing and watched his next move. He stepped into my cold fireplace, scratched aside some ashes, looked me straight in the eye, and pooped. He then covered his mess and left.

It was not an insult; it was a challenge. And by God, he picked the right man to confront. I could have simply cleaned the fireplace after every fire, but that would have been too easy.

Outhouses

That would have been surrender on my part. I bought a mess of mousetraps and scattered them strategically across the fireplace bed in such a way that it would be impossible for a cat—or a mouse for that matter—to enter that fireplace without incurring the wrath of one, or even several traps. I could only hope that Judy would come to meet his fate while I was there.

And so it was to be. Judy came in one evening as I was working at my desk. He paused and waited for my attention, which he got. I almost giggled in glee as he parted the metal mesh screen and stepped into the narrow firebox. Without much hesitation he walked in with all four paws, never so much as touching a trap. I was startled. He dug a hole in the ashes. Not a snap. I was astonished. He squatted and pooped without triggering a single slashing jaw. I was flabbergasted. He scratched a covering of ashes over his offering! Not one trap was triggered! I was livid with rage. He exited the fireplace, flicked some ashes from his paws, and looked me once again dead in the eye. And he turned and walked out of my office. I was drenched in respect.

Judy was not so lucky in his insulting dealings with my son Chris. Chris began to notice that about noon every day, while he was attending classes at the University of Nebraska, he began to take on a not very delicate aroma. It was apparently something with his shirts. They smelled bad once they had been worn for a couple hours. Not all his shirts. Just some of them. The ones, in fact, that were on the top of the laundry basket before the clean laundry went upstairs to be sorted out. Yep, Chris discovered that Judy made a point of peeing on Chris's laundry whenever it happened to be on the top of the laundry basket. No one else's. Just Chris's. Chris doesn't like cats. Cats know that. Judy knew that.

You can rub cats' noses in such offenses but it not only won't make a difference: They will then know they have succeeded in their perfidy and it will only encourage them. Daughter Joyce's cat started peeing in the kitchen sink. She knows and loves cats. She broke the cat instantly of that ugly habit by catching it once in the act . . . and praising it lavishly. There is nothing a cat hates worse than doing something praiseworthy. Her cat never peed in her sink again. Never. Cats cannot be reasoned with like a dog. You need to think like a cat and, in fact, out-cat them.

Chris did that, one of the few males alive to have ever accomplished that wonderful goal and I love him for that. He was once getting ready to take a shower and noticed Judy step into the shower stall. Chris reached back and slid the shower door closed. Now, I know what you're thinking. You're thinking what I thought: He turned on the shower and drenched that damn cat until it howled for mercy. But that would have only affirmed to the cat his triumph and he most likely would have taken to pooping in Chris's sock drawer, as our cat Hairball did to me moments before she was exiled from the house forever.

No, Chris thought like a cat. He knows that there is only one way for a cat to clean itself. With its tongue. So Chris opened the shower stall just a little bit, just enough to insert, well, to insert. And he peed all over that cat until there was no more fuel, so to speak. And then he calmly opened the door and invited the cat to leave. The cat never again peed on Chris's clothes, and what's more, he never did anything else along those lines either because he sure didn't want Chris pooping on him.

No dog would ever do anything like this, but I do know of a dog who loved to play at catching a Frisbee, but not as much as his "master" loved throwing one. So, the dog would get tired of the game but didn't quite know how to call an end to it. I mean, you can imagine. Dogs adore their masters and hate like sin to let them down. If you want to throw a Frisbee, well, any dog figures he should keep on catching it and bringing it back no matter how weary he is of this idiocy. So this guy's dog would simply approach the last Frisbee he intended to fetch and pee on it. That pretty much ended the game without anyone so much as having to say a word.

38
When You Care Enough
to Send the Very Best

I do know personally of one example of canines pooping in such a way that it constitutes a personal expression and I never see it without saying a quiet, "You're welcome, my friend." Don't tell my sheep-lovin' neighbors, but I am partial to coyotes. I sleep with my windows open just to hear their insane song, sometimes howled just a hundred feet or so from the house. My buddy Boom-John Carter once described them perfectly as "the Mormon Tabernacle Coyotes." And I do what I can to encourage coyote visits by hauling down an occasional sack of meat scraps or large ham bones or pizza crusts to the road down below our house and spreading them around in hopes it will that night constitute a coyote banquet, complete with a glee club entertainment. Most of the time the crows take what they can before the sun even goes down, and then I am almost certain the raccoons, possums, and skunks move in and help themselves to whatever is left. Most of the time there is nothing at all left by the time I get down there to take a look the next day.

But sometimes ol' coyote comes through and accepts my offerings. How do I know? Well, I hear his song during the night and know he is right there where I left the food, and other times on some very rare occasions during the winter I trudge down to the road the next morning and find huge, fresh canine paw prints in snow. But sometimes there is another sign, one that makes me laugh and makes me feel a special kinship with Mr. Coyote. He poops. Right there in the middle of the road. Right where I couldn't possibly miss it. In fact, more often than not, when I hear his song and know that he has been enjoying my gift to him, I can count on there being one of his little return presents down there too.

The coincidence of these events—food, song, and thank-you gift—are too consistent to be an accident. That is, I don't think those coyotes just happen to find the food, eat, and then poop. I know you're going to think I'm nuts, but I think those coyotes poop on purpose. For one thing, it is always right there in the middle of the road, or even closer, right up around the house, at the gate. Never just out in the grass, or up toward the highway, or down by the cabin, or out by the river. Nope, always in the road or up by the house.

If I'm wrong, I don't want to know I'm wrong so don't bother to try to talk me out of it. I like to think those little gifts are just that: personal messages, although perhaps a lit tle unconventional.

Public People Poopers

Although maybe not. Ask any experienced police investiga-
tor. A little-reported and therefore little-known bit of
crime trivia is the remarkable inclination on the part of bur-
glars to leave behind an expression of their gratitude or contempt or something at the scene of their crimes. In fact, this
curious behavior can become a factor in the very detection of
the crime. An item from the "[Police] Blotter" section of the
Lincoln *Journal-Star,* Tuesday, May 21, 2002:

> Lincoln police were called to an apartment on
> the 2100 block of E Street Sunday after a
> female resident reported a burglary.
> According to police reports, someone appar-
> ently entered the locked apartment, between
> 1 P.M. and 4 P.M., by unknown means, and
> stole a greeting card (value: $2). The woman
> told police she knew someone was there
> because the lid on her toilet was left up.

I am baffled by the meaning of the mixed message of this
police report. Only a man would leave a toilet lid up; only a
woman would bother stealing a greeting card.

40
Back to the Subject

But, where was I? Oh yeah, coyotes. My vision of this is Coyote coming across my presentation and noting from the traces of my own scent that it is indeed a deliberate gift and deducing from its placement right in his path, just where it so often is, that it is meant specifically for him. And of course he is right.

Then he eats the food and gets to thinking, "You know, most people are always chasing me away with their dogs, taking shots at me, trying to murder me with traps and poison, but this guy up in the big white house, he's all right. There must be some way I can thank him for his kindness. Let's see? What could I do? Well, I can sing a little baroque melody, something from Bach, the one with that particularly complicated soprano line." [Coyote sings two verses of "Fugue in F Flat." I know there's no such thing as an F flat, but if you've ever heard a coyote singing then you know that the mistake is one of western music notation, not of coyote composition.] "But I should do more. That prime rib bone was particularly fine tonight, especially with the side order of crusts of grilled cheese sandwich. What's to do? What's to do? What's to do?"

[Coyote exits stage right. Pause. Reenters just a few steps onto the scene.] *"I got it! I have just one thing that is completely my own, and I'll leave him some of that!"* [Coyote squats, shivers, and bobs tail up and down. Smiles contentedly. Exits again stage right.]

Outhouses

You're thinking, "How do you know it's coyote poop?" If you have ever seen coyote poop, you won't forget it. It never fails to make me laugh. It is dark, dry, wizened, and tortured. I'm not a pervert so I don't spend a lot of time fishing around in fresh coyote poop. I want to make that clear. No, I wait until it is a little drier and then I fish around in it. (Caution: this is not something you want to do lightly, I am told by experienced biologists. Animal feces can contain toxic fungi that can be inhaled and cause health problems. I'm not kidding on this.) And what I find over the years says a lot about coyotes. Over the years I've come to recognize owl poop, toad poop (no kidding), raccoon poop, skunk poop, possum poop, and for sure, coyote poop.

I have never found any chicken feathers, sheep wool, calf hair, blah, blah, blah, in coyote scat. The myth of coyotes preying on livestock is so much bullshit. Thing is, people whose lives are like prisons resent the wonderful freedom of Coyote and instead of fixing their own sorry situation do what they can to destroy things like coyotes. And eagles, and prairie dogs, and hawks and whatever else flies, runs, and swims free in this world. What I do find in coyote poop is little mouse and vole teeth, grasshopper wings, plum pits, watermelon seeds (Okay, okay, I will admit that coyotes are larcenous in that they do raid watermelon patches!), grass, and fish bones. If ever there were omnivores, it's gotta be coyotes.

41
For the Birds

Far more malicious in their dropping and leavings, I believe, are birds. There's nothing good to be said about the way birds poop. No way can you interpret their evil-doings as good-natured. There are always jokes about birds looking around for freshly washed cars, especially during mulberry season, but just as I believe coyotes use their feces in deliberate, communicative ways, so too do birds. I was once standing out in front of the University of Nebraska Student Union in Lincoln with a buddy, Rod. We were waiting for another friend, Walt, to come around and pick us up, so we were standing pretty much at the curb. And a bird pooped on Rod's head. Well, that's always good for a laugh, and we did, me more than him, perhaps.

And we looked up and saw a darkish bird sitting on the telephone wire directly above Rod, looking down as if in glee. Well, okay, it's pretty hard to detect glee in a bird's expression, so maybe we were reading something into the situation. I think it's called the "Romantic Fallacy," interpreting nature as if it had human emotions. It was just an accident.

Or maybe not. I used to joke at admiring our parakeet's ability to poop a little white dot and then encircle it just as neatly as a jelly donut with darker matter. (Of course I used to also delight in asking people if they knew what the white stuff was. When they said no, I would giggle with glee,

Outhouses

"Birdshit! Just like the black stuff!") But the bottom line, so to speak, is that that bird could poop that little donut, over and over again, and from altitude. Amazing, huh? Try this trick yourself sometime if you think this is no major accomplishment. Don't bother to send photos.

Anyway, Rod and I looked up and he said something to the bird, referring to its bad manners as I recall. But the bird didn't fly away, or even move on the wire. He just sat there, directly over Rod's head. So, being of sound mind, Rod moved. In fact, we both shuffled about 20 feet further away and continued our wait and conversation. And plop! Damned if another bird didn't poop on Rod's head!

Or was it another bird? We moved again and this time watched the bird on the wire. I am not joking here: That bird followed us down the line and once again positioned himself direction over Rod. Well, Rod didn't wait for that bird to generate another round of ammunition for his one-on-one shooting gallery, so we moved well away, not under a wire. And the bird flew away. But to this day, there is not a doubt in my mind that that bird pooped on Rod's head intentionally, not just once but twice, and would have done it again if we had continued to play his game. Moreover, I do not believe, even these 50 years later, that any bird "accidentally" poops on a human head or automobile. Birds know what they are doing, and they are way too good at it.

One of the richest memories of my life and of my father happened when I was a wee shaver working in our victory garden (if you are younger than 65, ask someone older what a victory garden was) and a bird pooped on his head. And it was mulberry season. I looked up at my pop with that ugly splotch running down his forehead and expected lightning bolts and thunder claps. I mean, jeez, this was my dad. And it was bird poop. Mulberry bird poop. Really ugly. But he pulled a big red kerchief from his back pocket, wiped at his head, looked up, and said something I have never forgotten: "For the rich, you sing."

Roger Welsch

I can think of only one time in my long life when bird poop was welcomed by the recipient. Our old rural mail carrier, Lyle Fries, was driving his route one day when a huge bald eagle flew overhead. Lyle watched that eagle swoop across the field in a line directly intersecting his own line of travel. Lyle scooched down in his seat so he could squint up through the top of his windshield to see the magnificent bird swoop just feet above his car. And right there in front of Lyle's eyes, while Lyle was carrying the federal mail, the bold symbol of our nation's greatness, a bald eagle, opened up and dropped about a half gallon of what could have passed for whitewash right onto Lyle's windshield. Actually, not just his windshield, but the whole blasted car. Imagine for a moment someone throwing a balloon bomb of white paint onto your car at high speed. Get the picture?

Well, anyone else might have been offended, but not Lyle. He thought it was a wonderful benediction. I don't know if that eagle knew Lyle well at all, or if he knew Lyle was delivering mail and was offering up some sort of spectacular acknowledgment, or was expressing a resentment about human intrusion. Whatever the eagle's intent, Lyle was thoroughly tickled. He came to town immediately after he finished his route and parked his car right smack in front of the tavern so everyone could get a chuckle out of that car so utterly bespattered with eagle shit. And he left the car so decorated for another week in case someone who hadn't been at the tavern that particular day wanted to take a look at genuine eagle shit before he had to wash it off. It was worth seeing.

42
Moo-Moo Doo-Doo

My Uncle Sam barn-broke his cows. Before going into the barn for milking, his cows stood outside the barn door, mooing and moaning, pushing and shuffling, trying to get rid of whatever they might have lurking in their digestive systems because for the next hour they wouldn't be pooping. Not in Uncle Sam's barn. He didn't allow pooping in his barn.

Believe it or not, a lot of old German farmers did that with their livestock. Why not? Cows are not stupid. They can learn. So why not save yourself a lot of trouble and work by having them leave that part of your job outdoors? In fact, a lot of old barns had a long wood or metal rod running across the tops of all the cow stalls, a foot or two above the middle of the cows' backs. Over each stall a vertical bar or to was attached to that crosspiece, usually with a thumbscrew or clamp so the vertical piece could be adjusted. And at the bottom of that vertical piece was a very sharp point. As they tell me—and believe me, I have been jerked around often enough by my country cousins that I sure wouldn't swear to anything they tell me!—a cow has to hump up her back just before she unloads, so whenever a cow in her stall got the urge and humped up in preparation, she was automatically stuck a good one right in the back. And she didn't do it any more. And no humping up, no pooping.

At least that's what they tell me. I know Uncle Sam's cows never pooped in the barn. At least I don't think they ever pooped in the barn. That's what my cousins told me anyway.

43
No Fuel like an Old Fuel

Cow poop has contributed to this nation's history, however, in more ways than you might imagine. The center of this nation might have remained unpopulated, unsupplied as it is without fuel for heat or cooking, if it had not been for the *bois de vache* . . . cow wood . . . cowchips . . . that cooked many a frontier meal and warmed many a pioneer family. As one old-timer told me many years ago, "Sonny, you needn't feel sorry for us cooking over cowchips. Didn't need any salt and pepper."

Plains Indians cooked over buffalo-chip fires for thousands of years and found it a perfectly acceptable fuel. It was clean, burned hot, did not smell, and certainly best of all, it was there! And there was precious little else to use as fuel, so it was seen as one of the many gifts of Father Buffalo. It didn't take pioneers long to learn that little trick, even though they managed to miss so many others, like drying meat, or gathering the bounty of wild foods available on the plains, or traveling light. Gathering dried cowchips became a major and lifesaving game in many plains pioneer communities.

Children were rewarded for bringing in the most chips, the best chips, the largest chips. A descendant of the children in one cowchip-fueled community once told me about how his ancestors began plotting in the spring in advance of the annual fall cowchip gathering festival. Over the summer they gathered fresh cow manure and in a safe, secluded place in the pasture where their work would not be discovered by other children or destroyed by milling cattle, they slowly, bit by bit (as it were) built the largest cowchip ever seen by man or beast. And come the day when all the children were sent out onto the prairies to gather the winter's fuel, this youthful cabal rolled their gigantic construction into the yard where the chips were being stacked into wagons. I am told that the parents were amazed, and then amused, but while they did give the inventive plotters a modest reward, they did not get the grand prize and were warned that the next year their entries better be closer to reason. And they were sent home to wash their hands.

Believe it or not, there was even a hierarchy of cowchip varieties in the pioneer fuel hierarchy. Especially prized, hoarded, and reserved for the long, bitter blizzard nights of the plains were the dried patties from cows that had been grazing in the plum, chokecherry, and sand cherry copses that are frequently found along plains creeks, rivers, and canyons. Cows eat the entire fruit, digesting the pulp but extracting and expelling the rock hard stones. When dried, I am told, these manure chips burned like coal—hot and long.

I am reminded of something I suppose doesn't really belong here. But then as I think more about it, I guess it really doesn't belong anywhere. So I might as well tell it here. Once my old buddy Bondo dropped by about the time we were sitting down to supper—funny how that seems to happen with Bondo—so he sat down with us and ate some of the wonderful fresh sweet corn they sell at roadside stands just down the road from my place. Garrison Keillor says that sweet corn is better than sex, and while I may not be prepared to go quite that far—of course I've never had sex with Garrison Keillor—I am partial to sweet corn. So, Bondo and I sat there at the table with butter and corn juice running down our arms and off our elbows until we couldn't eat any more. The next morning as I was walking home from town with the mail, Bondo pulled up alongside me in his pickup truck, rolled down his window, and without so much as a word of further greeting said, "You know, Rog, I really thought I chewed better than that."

44
Das Ist Ackerbau

To this day, smart farmers haul their animal manure to their fields to use as natural fertilizer and soil conditioner. I was once flabbergasted to find a lead story on the front page of the Omaha *World-Herald* about the dreadful problems of disposing of feedlot wastes throughout our cattle-raising state. I turned to page two to find another agricultural disaster story: the high costs of chemical fertilizers.

Duh . . .

I was traveling through Germany some years ago in an official capacity with a contingent of other dignitaries. I was the only one of the group who spoke German. As we passed by a field where a farmer was spraying a very smelly brown liquid from a large pump nozzle out onto his land, one of the ladies in the group, offended by the terrible smell, sputtered, "What is that?" The official escort from the German government pronounced, "*Das ist Ackerbau!*" ("That is agriculture!") Our less educated and more basic driver mumbled under his breath, "*Ackerbau! Das is Kuhscheiss!*" Even if you don't know German, you can probably figure that one out!

45
Talk About Constipation

If I had been a scientist, I imagine I would have wound up somehow studying the latter end of digestive systems. I suppose that says a lot about me, but not much good, huh? One of the finest, smartest, best, and funniest anthropologists I know is Alan Dundes of the University of California at Berkeley. He has made contributions to the understanding of mankind through his investigations of graffiti—or more precisely, latrinalia, or writings on the walls of toilets—and German attitudes toward poop. He has visited me here in my home. I kept wondering why he was taking notes.

Anyway, I am somehow attracted to this part of the process of living. I admit it. Okay, so quit pointing and laughing. A few years ago, a mountain lion wound up living down here along our river bottoms, just 100 yards or so from our back door. We heard her roar one night, and it was a sound I'll never forget. She lived here for two years, never bothering a soul, and then a half-wit with a gun and a badge shot her not far from here because, as he brilliantly noted, when he cornered her, "she got belligerent." The ignorant ass then had his photo taken with his kill on the tailgate of his pickup truck. Just what we want: a hysterical cop running around shooting things near the largest school in the area.

Anyway, during those years of her occupancy I told Linda on my frequent walks down to the river that if I didn't return on time, she should give the lion a couple extra days to finish up her meal before Linda sent someone down looking for me. Thing is, I explained, there's no way I'd rather exit this world than through a lion's asshole. I'd say that would add to my legend, huh? I told a friend of mine over at Game and Parks that if the lion did eat me, my wish was that he and some of my other friends would gather up a paper bag of the scat and place it on the altar at my memorial service.

"Nyah," he laughed. "That wouldn't be your style at all, Rog. You'd want us to take that brown paper bag full of lion poop, put it on someone's front porch, light it on fire, ring the doorbell, and run!" Well, okay, either way.

46
Everyone Loves
a Coprolite

Can you say "coprolite?" Last year I gave coprolites to some of my closest friends and favorite editors. I told them it reminded me of them. A coprolite is petrified dinosaur poop. I know it sounds unlikely, but think about it a second. There were a lot of dinosaurs, and all of them pooped, and I'm betting they pooped a lot. And just as some of their bodies, bones, and tracks wound up being buried in silt, sand, ash, and mud, so too did some of that poop. And just as I enjoy sorting through coyote poop to see what's been going on in Mr. Coyote's life, there are actually paleontologists—I wonder if they have a special name?—who study petrified dinosaur poop to learn what they can about that part of the creatures' lives. (For example, did you see *Jurassic Park*? The part where they sort through the Triceratops poop to find out what's wrong with it? Did you notice that the pile of poop is as big as the animal? Do you think that is likely? Have you ever seen elephant poop? Is it bigger than the elephant? Are movie directors idiots?)

And I just thought that hard old poop was appropriate for some of the people I know and love. To a soul they expressed first mystery, then appreciation. I usually explain that I went to a Web site where a computer will pick particularly suitable gifts: You simply feed in three words that describe the person who is to receive the item, and the computer does the rest. So, I tell my friends—or in some cases, those who were my friends—that I fed in the three most commonly used words to describe them: "hard, old shit"—and voilà! The computer came up with coprolites!

Some of these recipients still have those petrified turdlets in shadow boxes above their desks. And I still have a box of them here in my office, awaiting presentation to someone who strikes me as especially deserving. Let me know if you know anyone who particularly reminds you of very hard, very old shit and maybe we can fix them up with a . . . what is it again? . . . that's right . . . a *cop*-ro-lite!

47
Something Funny Going On

For as disgusting as we—and dogs—seem to find our processes of elimination, we also seem to find them funny. Almost as funny as sex, in fact, another bodily process we on one hand pronounce offensive but on the other find hilarious. To begin with, the processes themselves are funny. You don't even need a facility—privy, toilet, whatever—as a context. A friend of mine recently told through his own choked laughter about taking an elderly relative to the doctor for some tests. An attractive young nurse gave the old gent a little plastic cup and told him she needed a specimen, that he should pee in the cup. He looked at her and then the cup with some consternation. He held up his palsied hand and explained that he was never going to be able to hold the cup steadily enough to get anything into it. Would she maybe hold the cup for him? The nurse was appalled by the notion and made it clear that if he wasn't willing to take the chance of holding that cup, she sure as hell wasn't going to!

"Well, then" the old fellow grinned, "how about I hold the cup and you do the aiming?"

I intend to use that line myself in my old age.

One of the very first jokes I appreciated as a lad focused on this factor of our culture: A boy pushes over the family outhouse as a joke, only to learn later that Grandpa was using it at the time. As Grandpa approached the boy with a switch and a snarl, the boy thought back on his schoolhouse lessons and remembered that George Washington got himself out of a similar situation by admitting his guilt and preëmpting the punishment. So, the boy blurted out that he had indeed pushed over the outhouse. But Grandpa proceeded to thrash him anyway. When the boy sobbed, "But when George Washington admitted he cut down the cherry tree, he wasn't punished!" Grandpa replied, "Yeah, but George Washington's father wasn't in the cherry tree at the time."

That was hilarious when I was in junior high school. Years later, in high school, my sense of humor became far more sophisticated. Two guys are camping out in the wilderness one night, and one drifts off into the rocks to take care of a pressing need of nature. While he is squatting and admiring the stars, he feels a terrible pain in his nether regions and then hears the dreaded sound of a rattlesnake rattle. He staggers back to camp and blurts out to his buddy, "Man, I just got bit on the ass by a big ol' diamond-back rattlesnake. What'll we do?" Not knowing, his buddy tells him to remain calm, that he will begin at once the long trek back to civilization. The buddy runs cross-country through the night to the lights of a small village, hunts down the local doctor, and explains the situation. The doctor says he is in the middle of a difficult delivery at that moment and can't leave the mother and baby without care, but that he can explain briefly the simple process of dealing with snake bite: With a sharp blade, cut an X over each fang mark and then suck the poison out. The friend explains that well, uh, his pal was bitten in the ass. That's okay, the doctor says, that's the process that has to be followed.

The friend runs all the way back, cross-country, through the night to the campsite and falls exhausted by the campfire. The weakening snakebite victim says, "What are we supposed to do? What are we supposed to do?" to which the panting friend says, "The doctor says you're gonna die."

It must have been the Boy Scout influence. I found amusement in a lot of those outdoor pooping stories in those

Outhouses

days. A guy was telling some buddies about the most painful experiences in his long life in the wilderness—shot by Indians with multiple barbed arrows and pulling them out by himself. But that wasn't the worst thing that had ever happened to him. He was once torn to shreds by a grizzly bear and had to crawl back to civilization across 20 miles of nothing but rocks and cactus. But that wasn't the worst thing either. He was once out in the wilderness and went out into the night to poop, only to squat by accident over an open bear trap. The trap closed down on his testicles with viselike fury. "But," he said calmly, "that wasn't the worst thing that ever happened to me." His audience was stunned. What could be worse than that, they asked? "When I hit the end of that chain," he said stirring the campfire.

You see, a bear trap is secured to a tree by a chain. And when he jumped up, he. . . . Oh, never mind.

48
Meanwhile, Indoors

There are also plenty of modern jokes about modern facilities, especially public, multistalled toilets. Perhaps the most common traditional one is based on the all-too-common experience of using a public facility, only to find that there is no paper. A fellow in this situation hears there is someone in the next stall, so he says quietly under the stall divider, "Hey, man, you have any paper over there?"

"Nope. None here."

"Maybe a magazine? Or newspaper?"

"Nope. Not even that."

Long, long pause . . . "Well, then, uh, do you happen to have change for a twenty?"

I imagine that the appeal of stories along this line is that we have all found ourselves in a similar situation, or fear finding ourselves in a similar situation. A drunk staggers into a Catholic church and enters the confessional box. He sits down but says nothing. The priest coughs a few times to get his attention but the drunk just sits there, saying not a word. Finally the priest pounds three times on the wall to get his visitor's attention. The drunk sputters, "Ain't no use knocking. There's no paper on this side either."

Within the past couple weeks I was sent a story by e-mail about a woman who was using a public facility and a voice came from the neighboring stall, "So, how are you doing?" She was startled by a stranger offering a social contact in this otherwise private situation, but she decided to be civil and responded, "Just fine."

Voice in Next Stall: "Anything new with the family?"

Woman: "Uh, no, not really. Pretty much the same as usual. Kids are back in school."

Voice in Next Stall: "So, you're doing some shopping? What are you looking for?"

Woman: "I, er, well, yes, I am shopping, looking for some slacks, maybe some new clothes for the kids, socks for my husband. . . ."

Voice in Next Stall: (after along pause): "Excuse me, Marcia, I'm going to have to call you back later. Some smart-ass woman in the next stall keeps answering everything I'm saying to you."

Really long silence . . .

49
Out and About

I think I have established that toilets are funny and by virtue
of that inherent humor have become the subject of jokes.
But nothing is funnier than an outhouse. Yet even though I
am probably the only guy in my entire profession who still
uses an outhouse, all I have to do is mention the word *privy*
or *outhouse* in a social setting and I unleash a barrage of outhouse jokes and anecdotes. The memory does indeed linger.
Most involve the mysterious darkness down that hole.
Perhaps it's a Freudian thing, the hole representing some sub-
conscious trauma involving soiled diapers or some such
thing. I suppose that partly explains the faint-hearted attitude
some folks display toward outhouses. Indoor plumbing is bad
enough, with all that swirling and gurgling and roaring and
water disappearing into, well, who knows? But the deep, dark,
black hole of the privy?

Let's see, there's the story about the Bohemian fellow—
my wife's people—who is found fishing his overalls out of a
privy hole. When asked why, since they are obviously now
beyond any redemption as clothing, he explains that he did-
n't so much care about the overalls as he did for the kolache
in the pocket. (A kolache is an ethno-specific pastry that is
the very heart of Czech culture around here.)

Which is reminiscent of the guy who is spotted throwing
a $20 bill down the hole into the privy's pit. When asked why
he would do something like that, he explained that he acci-

dentally dropped a 50-cent piece down there, and while he sure as hell wasn't going to venture down there for such a pittance, $20 made the odious venture more than worthwhile.

I'm sure that the story about the old man abandoning a child that fell down the hole because "it's easier to make a new one than clean up the old one" must have comforted a lot of tykes already terrified about going out into that dark, lonely, stinky, dusty, threatening place.

I am—by training, profession, and inclination—a folklorist and have been for a half-century. And I know a little something about the persistence of tradition. It just does not go away! But I'll have to admit that even I am surprised when someone sends me a much-circulated story or joke involving an outhouse, when I would be willing to bet that not a single person on the long mailing list has ever had to use one, at least not in the last 50 years. Within the last two weeks someone sent me the old story about the farm woman who complains yet once again to her husband to "get out there and fix that outhouse." He can't get her, in her rural modesty, to say exactly what the problem is, however, so they both venture out to the privy so he can see for himself. "Well, I don't see a single thing wrong with this outhouse that a good sweeping and a little kerosene wouldn't take care of," he grumps. "What are you complaining about anyway?"

"Take a look down that hole," the wife instructs. He does but sees nothing. "Take a closer look." He gets down close and peers into the hole, directing his kerosene light down into the privy but still seeing nothing. "Get closer," she urges. He puts his face right down into the hole but still sees nothing.

As he rises and turns to her to question yet again what it is she is complaining about, a hair from his beard catches in a small crack in the toilet seat and is ripped out by the roots, bringing tears to his eyes. "Dang, but that hurts," he sputters.

"Now you understand the problem, Edwin," the wife says with satisfaction that she has made her case. "Fix the toilet seat."

50
You're in the Army Now

Nothing holds a candle to toilet humor. Human beings find toilets generally funny. Okay, male human beings find toilets generally funny. And nothing holds a candle to the humor potential in an outdoor privy. Or better yet, a military privy, indoors or out. And speaking of candles, someone—who the heck was it?—used to tell the story around here about an old gag in the Navy, where a ship's toilet consisted of little more than a trough with water running through it with dividers along its length to provide at least some privacy. A favorite trick was to wad up some toilet paper, put it into a preconstructed aluminum foil or wax paper "boat," ignite it, put it into the furthest up stream part of the sewage trough, and then listen to the howls of pain as the little fire boat made its way down the trough and under one bare ass after another.

After whoever it was told that story, my buddy Eric—now I remember this was his story—told about a time when someone dropped a lighted cigarette down an army slit trench privy and caused something of a furor. The privy was a building on skids, so a trench was dug and then the entire outhouse structure was slid into place over it. It was freshened now and again with commercial chemicals or kerosene or aircraft fuel and when it was full, it was simply covered and the outhouse was slid away to the next toilet site. Well, someone had decided that it would be way too much trouble to hunt up kerosene or commercial chemical, so he just sprinkled gasoline into the fetid slit trench. Lots of gasoline. So, then this poor wretch drops his cigarette into it. And, it being morning and all, every single stall of that privy was full when the gasoline went off. Twenty guys wound up with minor flash burns on their respective bottoms and experienced some chafing for the next few weeks, as their already sore bottoms dealt with the total lack of a hair buffer between their starched military ODs and the bare, burnt skin.

Now, that's really not all that funny, I know, but Eric said that what was really hilarious about this is that the fire department then had a heck of a time putting out the fire in the slit trench. But they did get it out eventually, dug a new trench, and moved the portable privy over it. I know, still not funny. But here's the funny part. All that fire had deposited a nice layer of oily soot on each and very toilet seat in that porta-privy and for weeks every enlisted man's bare ass in the shower sported a large, targetlike black ring around a much smaller but perfectly placed, uh, bull's eye.

Forty years ago I spent my obligatory military service of seven years in the Nebraska Air National Guard, and I learned one heck of a lot more than military regulations and job training! For a while I was a telephone installer. I would go with an advance team to whatever air base we were to occupy for our two weeks of summer service and set it up for the arrival of the main body of troops. In my case, that meant installing telephones and setting up the base communications system. The grizzled veterans freshly back from Korea made sure we fuzzy-cheeked newcomers learned the most arcane details of our job assignments. For example, it was SOP (Standard Operating Procedure) to install one spare telephone line into the offices of the Air Police, concealing it in the rafters, under a desk, behind a heating radiator. We would make a note of the telephone number assigned to that line and then attach an auto bomb to the end of it, hiding it well.

Do they even still make auto bombs? I suppose in these days of complicated electronics, you wouldn't even be able to find a spark plug wire to attach one to. Well, back in the olden times, for about 50 cents you could buy these things called auto bombs. You got under the hood of someone's car and ran one of the bomb's wires to a spark plug wire and the other to a ground somewhere on the engine or body. When the car was started, there was this horrific whistling-screaming sound, followed by a cloud of acrid white smoke, and then an explosion that sounded as if the engine had just been launched into orbit. Auto bombs were wonderful devices. I bet I spent half of my childhood allowance on auto bombs.

And we always took along a few auto bombs to Air Guard camp, specifically for the Air Police office. Sometime well into the weeks of summer encampment, when things had settled down to routine, a bunch of us would gather somewhere within sight of the Air Police building. Someone with climbers would scale a telephone pole, tap into a line, hook up a field phone, ring up the operator, and ask him to ring the number for that line we had tucked away many days before and tucked into the Air Police office rafters. If an auto bomb was startling under the metal hood of a vehicle, it was even more spectacular in the confined space and quiet of a police office. At this point the exercise became most dangerous for whoever had gone up the pole and made the call to the auto bomb line. Air Police would come rolling out of the smoke cloud pouring through the door of that building, fuming, cussing, coughing. If you were up on that pole, there was every chance in the world that you would get to laughing so hard, you would fall down and kill yourself from glee.

Now, what does this have to do with toilet humor, you're asking? Note that I said we took along auto bombs to guard camp. Yes, one was used in the Air Police offices, but another would be placed in the Air Police latrine. You simply cannot imagine how this lightened the burden of our military service.

51
Power Peeing

Only once did we wire up a urinal in this way. The floors of the biffies were perennially wet from being mopped by recruits, so it was fairly simple to run one wire of a telephone line to a urinal drain pipe and the other to a metal grate or simply to the floor of the wet bathroom floor near the urinals. The problem with this arrangement was mostly timing. It was easy enough to know when the Air Police offices were busy and full of personnel, but it would take some careful watching and cautious concealment to know when the urinals were in optimum occupation. But we were dedicated military men, and we were on duty, and we were ready to do whatever it took to do our job well. When an observer or educated guesswork led us to believe that a suitable number of our buddies were lined up in such a way as to complete the circuit, we would call the operator and have him ring the number of that urinal hookup.

I don't recall what the volts, watts, and cycles of our military telephones were. I get the impression it was something like a modern electric fence—not so strong as to be dangerous to the recipient, but a slow, pounding, insult to the body, for sure. And a special experience when part of the circuit included your penis. While I was never on the end, so to speak, of one of those military telephone calls, I was once duped by my farm cousin Dick into peeing on an activated electric fence. He told me if I did it, I would hear a sound I would never forget, and he was right—me screaming bloody murder, and then using words my mother would kill me for if she ever caught me using.

Same kind of words we heard coming out of the military toilets, as a matter of fact.

As of this writing I am 65 years old. To be perfectly honest, I cannot remember for sure if the above story about wiring a urinal ever actually happened. I know we rigged the urinal with the phone line, and I know we sat in our harnesses hanging from a telephone pole waiting for guys to go into that urinal, and I know we had that number rung up. But for the life of me, I don't know for sure if it actually worked, or if my memories arise only from my own delightful imaginings of what was going to happen and my long conversations with my buddy Paul Wurm about what was going to happen. Either way, I guess it worked out fine.

52
Wired for Action

I know for a fact I am not the only old fart whose aging memory operates like this. I recently had a long discussion with some friends, and we reminisced about the tavern in Lincoln, Nebraska, where there was a male statue in the ladies room, naked except for a fig leaf over the statue's naughty bits, as they say on the Monty Python show. When the leaf was lifted, an alarm went off outside the rest room in the tavern so everyone knew that the absent lady had an interesting curiosity. We also remembered that in the men's room there was an alarm on the condom machine. That was even more fun because it signaled some guy in our company had reason to think he was going to need protection later that same night, and often the lady generating that optimism was still sitting at his table waiting for him. We recalled the wonderful glow of embarrassment on the lady's face when the bartender announced what the bell ringing behind the bar was all about.

Now, as I said, that is our memory. The problem is, none of us can remember where that bar was. But we try not to probe too far in determining whether we only thought about how funny this scenario would be, or if it really happened. It's just too delicious a story to take that kind of chance with.

53
Of Men, Boys, and Privies

I was also a fraternity boy in my youth, something my later hippie compatriots find hard to believe. But I was. And there too bathroom humor prevailed. A bone of contention in our house was that the actives—full-fledged, initiated members of the group—had all the privileges and always took advantage of them. For example, when the cook made cake for dessert, the actives took all the chocolate cake and we pledges had to settle for the white. Eventually the time came in the spring when the pledges go on "sneak," running off and leaving the actives to do their own house cleaning, meal serving, and other menial chores. Late that Friday night, as we youngsters in the house gathered to leave for a football game in Norman, Oklahoma, we removed all the toilet seats and toilet paper from the bathrooms and drove off. On the long drive we burst over and over into gleeful laughter as we imagined the situation we left behind us. That night we had had a late dessert of cake. And the blasted actives took all the chocolate, leaving us the white yet once again. What they didn't know is we had made them a special chocolate cake for the occasion. A very special chocolate cake, frosted with Ex-lax. No toilet seats. No toilet paper. Lots of very active bowels.

Pulling plastic wrap tightly across a toilet bowl under the seat, so that when a lady sits and pees, it stops abruptly about an inch below its origins was so common it was almost traditional by that time. But there was another ugly little trick we would play on neighboring fraternities when they had parties scheduled. This was truly a dangerous assignment, but as I recall, we did bring it off at virtually every party. Often it was accomplished with the help of a cooperative girlfriend. When a fraternity threw a party, one or two of the several bathrooms in the house would be designated for the occasion as the ladies' room(s). The trick was to get into that room or rooms sometime during the evening and put two or three goldfish into the toilet bowl. Women would come into the room, look down into that bowl, and just not have the heart to pee on the innocent fish frolicking in the water below. Nor would they usually have the immodesty to tell any of the males of the house why they were getting more and more desperate as the evening grew longer. The hope was to bring about a very early evening's end for our friends next door.

One of the most memorable bathroom pranks I have pulled in my life turned out to be a surprise for at least three of us—including, as it turned out, me. I had a very fastidious buddy. And I had a box of practical joke junk I had accumulated over the years—plastic poop, soap that makes your hands turn black, phony bullet holes for a car window or bathroom mirror, that kind of thing. A bunch of us were going over to this friend's house for an evening of drinking and eating, and since we were pretty much a bunch of obnoxious louts to begin with, I tucked a really ugly splat of artificial vomit into my pocket, figuring I would put it on his bathroom floor sometime during the evening and he would figure one of us did it.

Well, I did, and it worked, sort of. I went into the house from the patio to use his bathroom, took the plastic vomit from my pocket, and put it by the toilet. This stuff was really ugly, and very realistic. Enough to turn your stomach. And then I went back out to the patio. Over the next hour three or four other guys went in and used the bathroom but they knew about the gag and so they said nothing when they came back. We all anticipated the golden moment when our host would go to use his bathroom, and eventually he did.

We sat there grinning and waiting. And we were rewarded. There was a loud explosion of curses from inside the house and out of the patio door roared our host, clearly and thoroughly agitated. With his cat in his hand. Which he launched in a splendid arc over the patio and into the surrounding bushes. Now, it was funny that he was duped by our gag, but nothing was as hilarious as the mystified look on that cat's face as he reached his apogee and neared the landing area in the honeysuckles. And then it really got funny when our host explained that his damn cat had been using the bathroom floor for a toilet all week, and this time had gone well beyond the limit.

And even that wasn't as funny as the sounds that came from the bathroom when he went back in to clean up the "mess," only to learn it was a piece of ugly plastic. And then there was the thought of him trying to get the cat to come home again that night. Frankly, I think this is why God put cats on this earth, for occasions precisely like this.

54
The Ultimate Joy
of the Outhouse

Nothing, absolutely nothing, arouses the adolescent sense of humor of the American male like an outhouse. Nothing. And it has always been that way. Our pioneer history is seasoned through and through with wonderful outhouse narratives, narratives that never reach the pages of our history books because, well, I don't want to make too much of why this kind of de-spicing of history takes place, but it does. A wonderful quotation usually attributed to Harry Truman tells it all: "The problem with history is that it's just one damn thing after another." And it is not just little old prissy female librarians and teachers who do this. In fact, quite to the contrary, it is my impression that it is mostly prissy old male historians who do it. History is actually wonderfully funny and salty, if we could just rescue it from the historians.

Anyway, over the years I have been told many an outhouse story, sometimes by the people who were involved, more often by those to whom the stories were given before me. There are the usuals, like outhouses tipped over at Halloween, but even that activity carries with it more import than the modern reader might understand. This was not just the inconvenience of setting it back up. On one occasion that I know of personally (but was not the victim of, I assure you) the owner was occupying the privy at the time it was tipped over. And it was tipped onto its face, which pretty much sealed the victim in it for the rest of the night. The worst-case scenario would be for the outhouse to be tipped over backward, and the owner to come out to take care of internal pressures in the middle of the night, not noticing the change in the skyline but simply following the well-worn path, falling directly into the privy pit.

Repeat victims of this kind of hooliganism would indeed sometimes move a privy three feet back off of its foundation during the early day of Halloween, thus inviting the vandals to approach the target and themselves to fall into the pit. That kind of triumph must have carried a wonderful sense of justice with it.

In Wales I saw stone-and-brick outhouses that would clearly obviate such activities, but I couldn't help but wonder how one moves a three-ton outhouse to a new location when that need arises, as it surely does. To this day, 40 years later, I regret not having asked.

55
Slow as Molasses

A common prank at pioneer social gatherings like square dances was "molassesing" the saddles. The thing is, when travel was by horseback or wagon, on rough roads and over rough country, gathering an extended community from substantial distances, it simply didn't make sense to travel all day to get to a dance at, say, six in the evening, dance a couple hours, and then turn around and travel six or eight hours to get home. So, the standard closing hour for any frontier social event was sun-up or as the day began to lighten.

There was no such things as baby sitters—you didn't leave your young'uns back home in the log or sod cabin while you went off dancing. After all, this was their chance for social contact too, so everyone in the family loaded up and went to the dance. Bachelors came on horseback for many miles away with hopes of meeting an eligible maiden on this rare but cherished event. The door would be taken off the house or barn where the dance was being held and used as a table for the foodstuffs everyone brought with them; potables were often discreetly buried into an oats bin or haystack nearby. The furniture was taken out of the house, the animals and machinery out of the barn, and the adults danced while the children . . . while the children got into trouble.

Sometimes a jug of molasses would be sneaked onto a wagon or carriage specifically for this purpose, but no homestead was without a molasses barrel, so it wasn't hard to put this prank together. On one occasion, the adults made a batch of taffy specifically to keep the children out of trouble. The adults figured the kids would be busy either pulling taffy or eating taffy and that would avert any problems. But it didn't work: the taffy never did "set"—get hard enough to turn into candy—and just stayed a syrupy goo, which was even better than molasses as it turned out.

During the night those too young to dance would carefully, quietly spread a thin, almost undetectable veneer of molasses on the bachelors' saddles. The morning star would rise in the east, the bachelors would bid a gallant adieu, leap to their mounts and ride off toward their homes. The horse knew the way home—probably better than the bachelor if they'd been visiting the oats bin or haystack—so the young man could drowse in the saddle as the horse took him unerringly home and into the barn, where the young swain would awaken to find himself solidly affixed to that saddle.

I have made a good part of my living as a banquet speaker, telling stories like this, which means that again and again I have been approached by people after such occasions wanting to tell me more about such events. One woman told me that her brother was thus molassesed. He awoke in the barn, firmly cemented to his saddle which was firmly cinched to his horse. He turned his sleepy mind to solving his dilemma: how to escape the sticky trap. She told me that he kicked off his boots, unbuttoned his pants, reached up to a beam in the barn, pulled himself up out of those pants glued to the saddle, kicked a leg up over the beam and thus extricated himself from his fix.

Only to find himself in another. Now, here he was, 10 feet above a pitch-dark barn floor, half naked. He couldn't just jump down among the machinery and tools and barn structures hoping for the best, so, his sister told me, they found him in the early morning, yelling for help. But not too loud.

And once after telling that story, another woman approached me and sniffed, "That was nothing. Think about the scoundrels who molassesed the privy seats at our church one Sunday during a congregational revival and picnic. It's one thing for a bachelor to yell for help from his family. But when you're a woman, at a church meeting, stuck in the privy. . . ." She didn't need to continue her story as far as I was concerned.

I have heard endless stories about hoodlums throwing firecrackers down a hole behind an outhouse shortly after someone enters, and there is always someone entering an outhouse, always a gap in the back between the structure and the ground it rests on, believe me. There is no guessing about this as there was in the case of me and Paul Wurm wiring the Air Police latrine! And I believe every one of these stories. But these days a new phenomenon has induced a sense of doubt that leads us all to doubt the fabulous. You know the stories: the cat in the microwave, the man with the hook on lovers' lane, the phantom hitchhiker. Jan Brunvand, a friend of mine but a man who needs help when it comes to labeling, has unfortunately called these "urban legends." They are a form of legend, a story taken to be truth, but they are no more urban than air. Thing is, Jan lives in Salt Lake City, which is urban; he heard the stories in Salt Lake City, which is urban; so he assumed the stories are urban. I hear them in Dannebrog, Nebraska, population 352. Unless Jan is goofier than I think he is, these stories are in nowise urban. They are, in fact, modern legends, as contrasted with the medieval legend. But, well, enough of that.

56
Excuse Me, Ma'am

Thing is, there are a lot of stories that circulate around here, possibly based in some truth, that are believed and enjoyed, and which serve as examples of surprise in a world where all too much is explained. You've probably heard the story: someone puts a speaker under an outhouse, often at a public event. The perpetrator lies in wait, watches for a woman to go in, waits a very carefully strategic amount of time, and then says into the microphone, "Ma'am, would you mind holding on just another couple minutes? We're painting down here."

First, does that strike you as being an urban legend? Write Jan Brunvand at the University of Utah and protest, if you are a rural dweller who demands representation. Secondly, well, let's face it: That's not real likely, right? I mean, you need a sound setup of some kind, and an outhouse, and someone willing to go to that trouble. It's a great idea, maybe even a great story, but what are the chances of it happening?

Well, I saw it happen. I am not claiming this is the origin of the legend. In fact, I know it isn't. My irrepressible buddy Marv Caspersen no doubt heard the legend, thought it was a great idea, and decided that he would indeed go through the trouble of engineering exactly this scenario. It was the grand Boelus, Nebraska, Fourth of July celebration in about 1976 or 1977. You can't imagine what those events were like. You wouldn't believe if I told you. They were the most flamboyant, fun, exuberant, authentic, hilarious, uninhibited, inventive American celebrations you can imagine. Now that I think about it, I should write a book about those wonderful occasions. They were some of the finest moments of my life. It was America at its acme.

Jeez, now I'm sounding like an old fart remembering the good old days, which isn't all that surprising, I suppose, because I'm at this moment being an old fart remembering the good old days. Anyway, on one of these Fourth of July celebrations I saw Marv sitting in the shade of a tree on the grounds of this blowout so I took a cold beer over to him and sat down on the ground beside him. He was intent on something and wasn't real eager to talk. I asked what he was doing. He glanced quickly at me, shushed me, pointed his eyes meaningfully at a microphone in his hand, and then off to an outhouse about 50 feet away, a line of women waiting at its door.

Oh God! No! It was happening right before my very eyes. This man was about to realize the adolescent dream, fulfill the modern legend! I knew instantly what he was up to and in utter fascination dropped down beside him. A woman went into the privy. Our stomachs tightened in anticipation as we tried to imagine the actions within to time perfectly what was certain to come next. We waited. I don't think we breathed. Marv looked at me meaningfully. We both looked back at the outhouse. He waited, perhaps a touch too long to my mind, and then he raised the microphone to his lips. He said the words: "Excuse me, Ma'am, could you hold off just a second until we finish painting down here?"

Unlike almost everything else in life—at least in my life—the result, some might say "consequences," were precisely as desired: the door exploded open, the woman came screaming out with one hand hitching up spinnaker-like panties, and the line to the privy dissolved in pained uncertainty. And Marv, half drunk, and I, way too sober, collapsed in near-convulsive laughter. I almost soiled myself and I didn't even need to go to the bathroom. It was simply so impossibly funny it was more than a simple human soul like mine could absorb. It was—no kidding—damn near an hour before I could control my body enough to walk. And I had to take special care not to encounter Marv the rest of that day, in fact, for months, because I would collapse in laughter. I prayed for a full year that I wouldn't meet him on the road while driving. The consequences could have killed us both.

57
The Eternal and Future Whoopee Cushion

Please don't bother telling me how infantile whoopee cushions are. As one of Antonia's favorite T-shirts reads, "I am not infantile, you stinky pants poopy butt!" Your admonishments mean nothing to me. There is nothing in this world funnier than a fart and that includes an artificial fart, i.e., whoopee cushion. But we all know the inherent faults of the traditional, rubber-bladder example: it was difficult to conceal because of its bulk, it went off and that was it—one shot. A substantial victim could blow a whoopee cushion apart like a truck tire on a freeway.

But this is a new age, my basal-humored friends! The electronic age! And the whoopee cushion has been swept along with all the other new scientific advances like the microwave oven, the computer, the calculator, and the Thigh-Master. I have watched the growth of this technology with the intensity of a true scientist. First, there was an electronic whoopee cushion that was much smaller and much stronger, set off by the pressure of a sitter. That was good. But then an even better development came along when I found a remote control whoopee cushion. It was placed in a suitable site and could be set off with an electronic, wireless trigger at the whim and will of the prankster. I couldn't imagine anything better. Other developments popped up, so to speak, now and again. I recall one that was set off by light; it could be concealed in a drawer, for example, or bathroom, and it fired off a woofer when someone opened the drawer or door or turned on a light. That's okay, but not very effective, to my taste.

The current state-of-the-art whoopee cushion is a long-distance—50 feet!—wireless unit with five different sound effects! I have reduced my simple-minded friends to total laughing shambles simply by setting the box in front of them and hitting the button six or seven times on the remote trigger. This thing doesn't even need a victim; just the sound alone can reduce a man to tears of laughter (and, curiously, a woman to sneers of disgust). I know better now than to think this is the end of the line. I am not an inventor or engineer so I can't even imagine what the next step is in the refinement of this wonderful device, but I have no doubts that in the future, hopefully before too long, we will once again be amazed by the genius of man's mind. In fact, is that the faint whiff of hydrogen sulfide I detect on the wind?

58
Writing on the Wall

Mene mene tekel upharsin is the writing on the wall. That's what the king found and asked Daniel to interpret for him. Daniel decoded it to say, "You are weighed in the balance, and are found wanting." Gulp. But the point is, even God writes on walls. And that's the way it has been forever. Archaeologists exploring the pyramids have found all kinds of graffiti (that's what it's called) that workers scratched into the walls. This graffiti was not the hieroglyphics that praise the pharaohs and gods. Instead it consisted of little ditties about what the foreman's wife does while he's at work, how badly Umhatphotep smells after a weekend of drinking millet beer, and how you should avoid the girls over at the Sign of the Sphinx Tavern if you don't want to wind up with a bad case of the crotch crickets.

There are entire books about the wall writings at Pompeii. Thing is, most archaeological sites slowly decay and fade into the soil but in the case of Pompeii, everything was buried just as it was at the time people were living there, so the very real things of life have been preserved, which includes graffiti. People are apparently driven to write their feelings, opinions, insults, thoughts, philosophies in public places. That, after all, is what the wonderful primeval paintings in the caves of Lascaux are all about: people writing on walls.

Roger Welsch

Maybe not just walls. There is a human predilection, it would seem, to express oneself in public. Who knows why? Perhaps it is the anonymity that is attractive. You can spout your idiotic ideas without having to deal with the consequences, for example. That is what most performance is about; even major and respected figures like Johnny Carson, Dick Cavett, or Jay Leno will tell you that. They are shy. They feel they are socially inept, or at least clumsy. So they perform, so they can project without interacting. I know this all too well because I am both a performer and a writer, which is precisely the same sort of noninteractive relationship.

59
Off the Wall

Through the 1960s and 1970s public expression turned to bumper stickers. Americans asserted their political feelings on the backs of their cars: "LOVE IT OR LEAVE IT." "CHANGE IT OR LOSE IT." "MAKE LOVE NOT WAR . . . OR GET MARRIED AND DO BOTH." This zinger form of debating has not always been a happy way to do things. More and more the statements became confrontational, insulting, abrasive, obscene. I don't know whether that was a reason American culture became so uncivil, or if American culture simply reflected what was happening anyway. Whatever the case, it happened.

What stunned me about bumper stickers was how clever they were. Obviously they were—are—always anonymous, and yet the humor struck me as pure genius. Some of my favorites from over the years:

"FORGET ABOUT WORLD PEACE—*VISUALIZE* USING YOUR TURN SIGNALS!"

"WE HAVE ENOUGH YOUTH—HOW ABOUT A FOUNTAIN OF SMART?"

"THE CHRISTIAN RIGHT IS NEITHER."

"WANTED: MEANINGFUL OVERNIGHT EXPERIENCE."

"I LIKE CATS—LET'S EXCHANGE RECIPES."

"A PBS MIND IN AN MTV WORLD."

These days you almost never see a bumper sticker except maybe on a pickup truck. I imagine it's a matter of permanence: The modern American automobile's bumper is not strong enough to sustain for very long the weight, not to mention the impact of an opinion. Most pickup trucks—at least mine—use the bumper sticker as a device to hold the poor vehicle together. So, now the billboard for personal statement, invective, insult, or irony has become the T-shirt! Again and again, I am astonished by the genius of these things. How can writing be so bad for television but so great for T-shirts? Who does this? Is it one or two brilliant philosophers who keep cranking out one great line after another, or do we each get one shot at a great line, and some of these one-off gems make it to the public forum of the T-shirt? Beats me. I consider that one of the great philosophical questions of our time.

My own favorite T-shirt was sent to me by the owner of a transmission shop in Florida: "WE CHEAT THE OTHER GUY AND PASS THE SAVINGS ON TO YOU." I think that's hilarious. Linda and Antonia's favorites are:

"I USED TO HAVE TROUBLE FINISHING THINGS BUT NOW I. . . ."

"I AM IN SHAPE—ROUND'S A SHAPE."

"I FOUND JESUS—HE WAS BEHIND THE COUCH THE WHOLE TIME."

"WHAT IF THE HOKEY-POKEY IS WHAT IT'S ALL ABOUT?"

"TEN THINGS MEN KNOW ABOUT WOMEN:
1. 2. 3. 4. 5.
6. 7. 8. 9. 10. THEY HAVE BOOBS."

Another, obviously from a woman:

"WWXD?" [WHAT WOULD XENA DO?]

"JESUS IS COMING—LOOK BUSY!"

"THE GENE POOL COULD USE A LITTLE CHLORINE."

"FRIENDS DON'T LET FRIENDS DRIVE GREEN TRACTORS."

"WOMEN WHO WANT TO BE EQUAL WITH MEN HAVE NO AMBITION."

"OH NO! NOT ANOTHER LEARNING EXPERIENCE!"

60
Latrinalia and Literature

For the purposes of this volume, however, I am interested in one particular kind of writing: that which is inscribed on bathroom walls. I believe that a special category in this book and in the field of anthropology is deserved because I think it is especially significant. In fact, I think this kind of folklore deserves a special category and special attention even within the area of literature. For many years I taught within an English Department, a very good department within a major American university. My office was on the lofty third floor of the building housing that department. One could presume that anyone using the bathrooms in that building, and especially at that floor, was at least a student of the literary arts, probably a graduate student, maybe even a faculty member.

I made a point of visiting the bathroom in that building every day I was there, not because I have a weak bladder, which I don't, but because I wanted to catch up on the news, scan the public pulse, enjoy the best of creative writing . . . on the walls of the toilet stalls. Again and again I looked at my students and colleagues and wondered who the hell were the creative geniuses who inscribed the brilliance on the toilet stall walls while writing such totally execrable crap in essays, papers, reports, bulletins, memos, and announcements. Now that I am no longer teaching, I still wonder that I am surrounded by such utterly inarticulate boobs—is there anyone so utterly incapable of linguistic expression as the American, for chrissake?—

when wonderfully thoughtful, meaningful, comedic, terse, poetic gems appear again and again on the bathroom walls these same idiots frequent? Now and then I truly ponder if maybe the writings on the wall are not put there by the same author Daniel interpreted. Which is not so much a reflection on the readers as the author, I should make clear.

In fact, the distinction between ordinary scribblings on ordinary walls and the literature that appears on bathroom walls is so significant that a word has been coined for the genre by the folklore-anthropology genius and nose-tweaker Alan Dundes: "latrinalia," an infinitely better coinage than "urban legend." And what a grand category it is. For one thing, it is universal: I'm betting there is not an American alive who has not seen writing on bathroom walls at one time or another. And I'm betting there is not a fragment of our population who has not appreciated it. And only a few less who have not laughed out loud in the solitude of the most solitary of human activities when reading it. And, most notably, few who have not been moved, troubled, inspired, or stunned by it.

As I understand it, the title of the theatrical piece *Stop the World, I Want to Get Off,* was inspired by a toilet scribbling. As was *Who's Afraid of Virginia Woolf?* I'm not talking here about the scribblings of "For a good time, call . . ." or the random, unadorned obscenity. I think it is interesting that people are moved to such expressions but for the sake of brevity in this section of a book meant for short-term reading, I want to concentrate on the truly creative, inspiring, witty *mots* that occasionally grace us in our toilet wanderings and tarryings.

61
The King

While I was writing this section, I asked a bunch of friends for their favorite graffito, especially latrinalia. John Walter of *Successful Farming's* cyber department noted that it might take him a day or two to come up with his favorites, but he could recommend to me a short story by Stephen King that appeared in the *New Yorker*. Hmmm. Pretty fancy readin' for a book about outhouse literature! But with the help of other friends, I ran down the piece, "All That You Love Will Be Carried Away," originally appearing in the January 29, 2001, edition of the *New Yorker*, but also reprinted in a collection of King's shorter work, *Everything's Eventual: 14 Dark Tales* (Hodder & Stoughton, 2002). King's story reveals a lot about latrinalia, with some fair-to-excellent examples (the title is presumably a bit of graffiti the principal character has collected from Walton, Nebraska, just west of Lincoln), but even more about our own fascination with writing on bathroom walls and its creativity. King shows his own fascination with toilet stall philosophizing, asking the questions we all have about who comes up with this stuff, what it means, and why some of it is so fascinatingly obscure and riveting. As examples of their stunning literacy, poetry, and obscurity, King offers:

"My mother made me a whore," to which another writer had added "If I supply the yarn will she make me one?" (Casey, Iowa); the exotic meter of "Here I sit, cheeks

A FLEXIN', GIVIN' BIRTH TO ANOTHER TEXAN," which King accurately described as "an oldie"; "NOBODY HERE EVEN IF THERE IS" in Chalk Level, Missouri; "POOPIE DOOPIE YOU SO LOOPY" from Papillion, Nebraska; and as stated, the title of his story, "ALL THAT YOU LOVE WILL BE CARRIED AWAY."

In fact, King's protagonist Alfie Zimmer considers publishing a semischolarly anthology of his seven years of collecting writing from bathroom walls across the countryside but in the end is even embarrassed about the possibility of someone finding his notes after his death. Who but a lunatic would collect writings from bathroom walls?

Who but a folklorist? Or maybe a gourmet foods salesman interested in the world around him and stuck in Nebraska during a blizzard?

62
Poopie Doopie

As a folklorist I am more than interested in the traditional items we find on bathroom walls, and let me note here that contrary to what most men think and most women insist, women's toilets are at least as adorned and inspired as men's. I have had students do surveys and studies that convince me this conclusion is a true one. In fact, as with T-shirts and bumper stickers, bathroom walls seem to be a principal arena for the war between the sexes.

"WHY ARE YOU LOOKING UP HERE? THE JOKE IS IN YOUR HAND," or alternatively "WHY ARE YOU LOOKING UP HERE? YOU'RE PISSING ON YOUR SHOE," is obviously a male-specific bit of latrinalia, as are "STAND CLOSER—IT'S NOT AS LONG AS YOU THINK" and "WE AIM TO PLEASE, YOU AIM TOO, PLEASE."

"DO NOT THROW TOOTHPICKS IN THE URINAL; CRABS CAN POLE VAULT" is a standard, but more inventive and less common is one of my own favorites, "PLEASE DO NOT EAT THE URINAL CAKES."

"WE DO THEREFORE WE BE: NIETZSCHE . . . WE BE THEREFORE WE DO: KANT . . . DO BE DO BE DO: FRANK SINATRA" is, on the other hand, nongender specific, as is the delight I once found in a university men's room in a building shared by the English and Classics departments: "COITO ERGO SUM." (For those of you who don't speak Latin—and let's face it, most of my readers don't—Descartes' philosophical conclusion was "Cogito ergo sum," "I think, therefore I am." "COITO ERGO

SUM," with the elision of that one small letter in the first word, becomes, "I screw, therefore I am." Very highbrow stuff.)

It is understandable that one would find intellectual toilet scribblings in an English Department bathroom but it was in a New York subway toilet that my nominee for the cleverest graffito of all appeared. A public service sign encouraging literacy was ever so slightly defaced with two very small, otherwise insignificant dashes of ink by someone with a devilishly clever mind so that it no longer read: "THE PEN IS MIGHTIER THAN THE SWORD." Thanks to the graffiti artist's small changes, it read: "THE PEN-IS, MIGHTIER THAN THE SWORD."

An absolute classic of this category is one I'm betting I can start and you can finish, thus demonstrating its universality: "HERE I SIT ALL BROKEN HEARTED. . . ." See? And isn't it curious, while we're here, that people who have probably never otherwise uttered, yet committed to memory, a single stanza of poetry, do seem inspired by doggerel of this kind to memorize at least this? Maybe it's simply that this is a moment in otherwise busy lives when we have time to consider poesy, but I think there also has to be inspiration within the motivation. In preparing this part of this book I asked a wide range of my friends for their favorite graffito, preferably latrinalia. I am willing to bet that if I had asked them for their favorite poem, most would have simply shrugged, some might have started "There was a young man from Nantucket . . ." maybe a few show-offs would have actually been able to recall a couple lines from something they were forced to memorize in high school. But every single one of them had a particular favorite from a bathroom wall somewhere, and everyone was reduced to uncontrollable laughter even as they told their choice to me.

[Written in very small letters on the bottom of the stall door]: "YOU ARE NOW SHITTING AT A 45-DEGREE ANGLE!"

"IF ASSHOLES COULD FLY, THIS PLACE WOULD BE AN AIRPORT."

Outhouses

"HOT TAMALES—THE ONLY FOOD KNOWN TO MAN TO LEAVE AN EXIT WOUND."

Without question however my favorite latrinalia which I have seen myself was in a men's room in a truck stop just east of Council Bluffs, Iowa, where someone had laboriously scratched into the face of a condom machine, "THIS GUM TASTES LIKE RUBBER." That one knocks me out to this very day. (A much inferior variant of this is used by King in his short story; he should check with me next time he writes something for the *New Yorker.* A certified folklorist would be a valuable asset for him.)

63
Eric's Retirement Fund

An item of latrinalia with an interactive mode and interest-ing conclusion was found right here in the men's room of the tavern in my little town of Dannebrog. Eric was the pro-prietor and bartender, and someone scratched on the wall above the urinal "ERIC'S RETIREMENT FUND," with an arrow pointing down to the urinal, where the author had tossed a few now-bepissed pennies. Over time, the idea caught on and more and more pennies appeared at the bottom of the urinal. Once very couple weeks Eric took on the disgusting chore of fishing the handful of well-patina-ed pennies from the urinal, never saying a word, probably hoping the adolescent game would sooner or later lose its amusement for his customers.

But it didn't. For many months, pennies continued to accumulate in the urinal and long-suffering Eric (presum-ably) fished them out. Until one night after the urinal had been freshly cleaned and the "retirement fund" collected by Eric. As all my cronies—clearly the perpetrators of this dis-gusting prank—settled in for an evening of beering, Eric brought the first round of frosty, cold mugs of beer to the table, each with a stained penny lying in the bottom. That was the end of "Eric's retirement fund."

If you feel you have been cheated in life by not having access to the finer wall literature, you might take a look at the Web site www.bathroomjokes.com. I'm not kidding. Is there any facet of life whatsoever that doesn't have its own Web site these days? Well, certainly not latrinology. . . .

64
The Beat Goes On

Excuse me. I need to step outside for a moment to, uh, get some firewood. Be back in a minute. Unless I get tied up watching the deer down by the river, or counting clouds, or checking the lingerie pages in the Sears catalog (actually, these days it's more often than not the Sears tool catalog!), or chatting with the skunk that lives in the "basement," or thinking about something philosophical like the meaning of life.

I can assure you of one thing, however: When I come back, I will be refreshed and renewed. I will have taken a nice walk, enjoyed some of God's wonderful nature, rested for just a moment in my busy day, reminded myself I am after all an operating machine, that there are some things I have in common with all my fellow human beings all around the world. No matter what our differences, this one thing—this one thing—we have in common. Hey! What the heck—I have a two-holer. There's plenty of room. Why don't you just come along and join me? I've got some great stuff to show you, some stuff someone wrote on the wall. And sometimes this 13-stripe ground squirrel comes around while I'm, uh, resting out there. And on page 356 of the Sears Catalog there's this babe in the nightgown section that will knock you out. . . .

Better yet, why not drop me a line, either at Rural Route, Dannebrog NE 68831 or e-mail to privyguy@hotmail.com.

Afterword
More for the Glutton

"What is man, when you come to
think upon him, but a minutely set,
ingenious machine for turning, with infinite artfulness,
the red wine of Shiraz into urine?"

—Isak Dinesen, *Seven Gothic Tales*

It has always amazed me that whenever I have launched off onto a project like this—tall-tale postcards, sod houses, old tractors, love and romance—before long I am buried in letters, calls, and (these days) e-mails from people who have something to contribute to the dialogue. That has happened with outhouses, in spades. In the above text I mentioned Wright Morris's brief essay about outhouses in his book *The Home Place* and Stephen King's short story in the *New Yorker*, "All That You Love Will Be Carried Away," but there is so much more that those of you who have an abiding interest in our "private places" should be aware of. For example, do you know there is a major outhouse museum and hall of fame? Yep, The Connie Denault Outhouse Collection, which was donated to the West House Society for permanent display at the Outhouse Museum at the Rossignol Cultural Centre in Liverpool, Nova Scotia. Man, would I ever like to make a pilgrimage there! Curiously, I am writing these words on August 2, 2002, and the Museum opened for business on July 30, less than a week ago!

Outhouses

Sherman Hines, the eminent outhouse photographer, has his collection at the same site, and he offers a newsletter for the privy scholar, *The Outhouse Preservation Society Newsletter.* He also puts out an annual calendar of outhouses. You can check into that at the Outhouse Preservation Society Newsletter, RR2 Newport, Nova Scotia, Canada, BON 2AO.

Perhaps the king of outhouse Web sites is "The Official Outhouses of America Tour" at www.jldr.com/ohindex.shtml. This site contains a world of information about outhouses, but best of all, links to many other sites of interest, including outhouse preservation sites in other parts of this country and abroad. I know—amazing! You can find out more about the Bonnie Denault Outhouse Collection and Sherman Hines at: www.outhousemuseum.com/denaultcollection/denaultcol-lection.html.

A more modest site but with some interesting informa-tion is "The Outhouse" at www.cyberenet.net/~kelta/out-houses.html. "Primitive Plumbing: Outhouses Are In" is help-ful, with links to other sites and some bibliographic informa-tion for books about outhouses. "The Story Behind the [Famous WPA Outhouse] Button" is a personal Web page of a collector of outhouses and outhouse materials, including another version of the story about the government-issue privy being named after Eleanor Roosevelt and official plans for it.

The "personal place," as a Nebraska farmer once alluded to it while trying to avoid being any more specific, has rarely been celebrated or recognized with its own monograph. I am proud to note that I composed the introduction for one of the best of modern studies, *Ode to the Outhouse,* published by Voyageur Press, with generous photos and illustrations (2002). This slim volume is a delight, as sales have shown, and belongs on the shelf of anyone who considers himself—or herself, in those rare circumstances where the outhouse admirer is a member of the distaff—a true fan.

A couple fairly obscure, maybe even out-of-print items can be found on Web auction sites since they were printed in enormous numbers are Mahlon N. White's *Pretty Privies of the Ozarks,* published by the Democrat Publishing Company in Clinton, Missouri 64735 (no date) and Makin Wynn's (surely—surely!—a nom de plume) *Of Pots and Privies: From the Chronicles of Makin Wynn* (Denlinger's, Middleburg, Virginia, 1959). The absolute classics of the field, without doubt, are *The Specialist* and *I'll Tell You Why: Sequel to The Specialist* by Charles "Chic" Sale (Specialist Publishing Company, Carmel, California, 1929 and Western Newspaper Union, Wainwright Building, St. Louis, Missouri, 1930). These latter two are the *sine qua non* of privy reading and scholarship. You shouldn't even have *this* book if you don't have at least *The Specialist.*

The Sanitary Privy, Environmental Health Bulletin 4-3 issued by the Division of Environmental Health, Kansas State Department of Health in June 1974, is a rare gem. This is a precise and serious guideline for the construction of the very finest of privies. If you are serious about building yourself a rural chapel, you have to find one of these publications and study it like the Bible.

There are probably better books about latrinalia than Allen Walker Read's *Classic American Graffiti* (Maledicta Press, Waukesha, Wisconsin, 1977, originally published in Paris in 1935 privately to avoid the hapless and hopeless prudery of America at the time). I suspect that my own attraction to this book is because I met Read in the mid-1960s and heard him read a scholarly paper about graffiti at a Denver meeting of the American Folklore Society. He was a delight and his scholarship was more of a performance than a reading. He brought down the house—the outhouse.

Love, Sex,
and
Tractors

*The following is an excerpt from
Roger Welsch's best-selling book* Love,
Sex, and Tractors. *It is available from
MBI Publishing. To purchase a copy,
call 1.800.826.6600, or else visit our
website at motorbooks.com.*

*Remember what Shakespeare said about romance.
No, wait a minute—it was Sherman. And he said it about war.*
                                        —Anonymous male

Okay, let's get this chauvinism thing on the table and settled before the first cards are dealt: I am an accomplished and experienced male chauvinist sexist pig. This book
is for men only, and that's it. You can call me names if you
want (bet you can't think of a new one) and you can take me
to court but if you're a woman and you read past this point
{*}, I'm not going to be responsible for the consequences.

Roger Welsch

My first tractor book was *Old Tractors and the Men Who Love Them* (MBI Publishing, Osceola, Wisconsin, 1997) and it was made darn clear to me within moments of publication, while the ink was still warm and wet, that I had committed a major error in gender etiquette. There are women, I was told, who also love old tractors. And there are. So I apologized. Only to find out later that the selfsame women who protested my lack of diplomacy and narrow male view of things were buying the book specifically out of a prurient interest, lustily attracted to the inadvertently—but apparently irresistibly—undone side buttons on my overalls in the cover photograph. (I also learned that bookstore clerks were shelving the book among the romances because they mistakenly thought that was Fabio draped over the radiator of the Allis Chalmers WC!)

Later I wrote a book titled *Diggin' In and Piggin' Out* (Harper Collins; New York, 1997), where I tried to make it as clear as I could that the book was meant for men. The publisher in that case would not print the gender requirement on the cover however—something to do with the Constitution—and as a result, information about the most intimate details of the male psyche fell directly into the hands of women who probably used it in ways I don't even want to think about.

For example, in that book I revealed that, contrary to the female notion that frilly and silky things like Victoria's Secret underwear drive men crazy, it is actually mashed potatoes that do the trick. I have since heard three reports, one even in Nebraska, where women who illegally bought the book and, unrestrained by natural and international rules of romance, have combined Victoria's Secret underwear with mashed potatoes resulting in a kind of Cupid's neutron bomb, rendering unsuspecting males utterly incapable of defending themselves in matters of the heart.

I hold myself responsible. I don't want that kind of thing to happen again. So, this book is restricted, for male eyes only.

Love, Sex, and Tractors

This is not unfair. Far from it. Actually, I am only balancing the scales once again. Up until now it is women who have held the clear advantage, in large part unfairly gained. This book is only an honest, open, and legal way to even the field. I am astonished how many men I encounter who do not know about Woman School. Boys, there is such a thing as Woman School. You're an idiot if you think it is just a coincidence that all women do exactly the same things, say exactly the same things, demand exactly the same things, complain about exactly the same things, and uh, offer exactly the same things, if you catch my drift there on the last item. Mothers and daughters, old and young, far and wide. They're all alike because they've all gone to Woman School.

Don't bother to ask the women in your life about Woman School. They will either categorically deny there is such a thing or smile a peculiar kind of what-idiots-you-men-are smile. There is a school of thought in the art world, in fact, that just before Leonardo da Vinci painted the Mona Lisa, he asked her, "Do you-a know anything-a about-a disa Woman School-a, Mona?"

I know what you're thinking: if there is such a thing as Woman School, when do women go there? Where is it? Why don't we notice that they are gone when they go to Woman School? It's all around you, every day. That's what they do when they all go together to the "ladies room" at the same time. Do you actually believe it takes women that long to pee?! Get serious! They're in there holding a seminar on "Confusing The Idiots" or "Giving Driving Directions from the Passenger Seat" or "Packing a Purse" or "Unreasonable Demands," that's what they're doing.

Walk into a crowded Ladies Room sometime and see what happens. Do you think they're getting that excited because you caught them putting on lipstick or cleaning their glasses? No, your unexpected appearance in that inner sanctum threatens the security and secrecy of Woman School.

I should perhaps note here that this may not be some-thing you want to bring up in mixed company since many women carry their denial of the existence of Woman School right up to the thin line between insistence and violence. Once up at Eric's Tavern I was outlining these contentions about there being a Woman School for a bunch of buddies, all of whom I might add were banging their chins repeatedly on the bar in their enthusiastic nods of agreement.

Just as I finished up and revealed my inside information about this issue, Patty Stoeger, who had been uncharacteristi-cally quiet up to this point in a booth pretty much out of sight of the main seminar, then muttered loud enough for all of us to hear, "I guess that means you guys must have all gone to Asshole School."

This slim volume is an effort to correct the imbalance, to create a kind of Man School, as it were, no matter what insen-sitive women like Patty Stoeger might call it. Women will hate this book, not because they are excluded, not because it is crude and insensitive, but because it challenges the exclusivi-ty of gender training.

So, fair warning, gents: if you don't want this book to dis-appear mysteriously, hide it under the seat of your pickup truck. Tuck it back behind something sharp and dirty in your shop. Disguise it with a dust cover from a book by Dr. Laura or Danielle Steele. Put it some place where the woman/women in your life will never see it—tape it under the toilet seat. Disguise it as a car that is way overdue for an oil change. Keep it under the cover of your barbecue grill; she'll never see it there. Am I serious? Boys, listen up close—my wife Linda has not read this book. As my pal Eric says, "I may have been born on a Saturday, but it wasn't last Saturday."

Wise in the Ways

So, why not a book just about love, romance, and women? What's the deal with tractors? Thing is, it is generally a good idea for writers to write what they know about. But not what they know too much about. Have you ever read an encyclopedia? Of course not. Guys who write encyclopedias know too much. You don't want to know everything when you read a book; you just want to know something. A friend of mine once asked a lawyer to write a document for him and the lawyer told him the charge would be $4 a word. My friend thought the situation over and said, okay, but he would only pay him $4 for words he didn't already know himself. In other words, four-dollar words.

But my problem is that you already know a lot about women, love, and romance, probably even a lot about tractors. Maybe even more than I do. About tractors, anyway. But I'm not like the lawyer. Linda and I were once up at the local tavern talking with my two buddies, Woodrow, a plumber, and Lunchbox, an auto body repairman. I mentioned that I was writing something for Esquire magazine. My pals wondered how I get paid for writing something like that. I said, well, sometimes I'm paid so much for an article, agreed on beforehand; sometimes I'm paid by the word; a couple dollars or fifty cents or whatever per word.

"You mean," said Lunchbox, "every time you say 'the' they give you two dollars?"

"Yeah," I said. "That's the way it works."

While the boys were still reeling from the information that I am sometimes paid for writing words even they know, Linda, sensing their confusion, leaped to my rescue. "He gets paid for using the same words over and over," she explained. "But he has to put them in different order every time."

So, here they are. Same words, different order. I am not suggesting, by combining them between the same covers, that women and tractors, romance and restoration, are alike. No, tractors and restoration are much easier, more gratifying, more fun, cheaper, quieter, easier to get along with, and something you can do with your buddies on weekends. Nor do I mean to imply that I know as much about one as the other. But I do have a pretty good idea of what I don't know about all of the above.

Roger Welsch

Old Tractors and the Men Who Love Them plucked a string on America's psychological banjo, all right. Men and women from all over the country wrote me, sent me tractor signs and parts bags and chocolate-chip cookies, telling me stories about how their fathers had loved an old tractor, about how they have an old tractor they hope to get going one of these days, how pissed they are that their granddad let his old machines go up for sale at an auction instead of leaving them to the grandkids in the will.

For one thing, I was writing about something pretty fundamental—old machines (not me, the tractors), second, I was speaking from my heart and not my brain, and finally, I used plain English and none of that high-falutin' technical crapola. What people are saying to me is not that they learned a lot of new stuff from *Old Tractors* or *Busted Knuckles* but that I told them what they already knew. They weren't excited about acquiring new information; they were relieved to find out they aren't the only doofuses (or maybe the word is "doofi") in the world of rusty machinery.

That's the way it is with me and sex and romance too. If you want to find out something new, check out a copy of the Kama Sutra. We still don't understand the old stuff, yet we should try to figure out something new. After all, isn't the most common gender-based stand-up comedy routine still the one about men leaving the toilet seat up and women being boiled about that? Why is that still funny? Because everyone is still deeply involved in the toilet seat up/toilet seat down wars, that's why.

Women, probably for all the remaining time until the world collapses into a frozen wad of ice, slag, and disposable baby diapers, will snarl about how inconsiderate it is for a man to leave a toilet lid up when he's done using it; up until pretty much the same moment, all men will remain utterly baffled. Only women get angry about this. Men just don't understand why it's such a big deal to check a toilet seat before you sit down on it. How can a woman be so fussy about whose lap she sits on and so careless about dipping the same equipment into a toilet bowl?

A female friend, Cheryl, has offered the only reasonable explanation of this curious insistence on Lid Up I have ever heard: she says it's a matter of approach. Driving down the highway at 60 miles an hour is one thing, she explains, but backing up to park is done with considerably more care, because there is considerably greater chance for mishap. Not bad, but still, why not just look at the blasted thing when you come in the door, Cheryl?

Other books by Roger Welsch:

Busted Tractors and Rusty Knuckles
ISBN 0-7603-0301-0

Everything I Know About Women
I Learned From My Tractor
ISBN 0-7603-1627-9

Love, Sex and Tractors
ISBN 0-7603-0868-3

Old Tractors and the Men Who Love Them
ISBN 0-7603-0129-8

The Tractor Trilogy
ISBN 0-7603-1305-9

Index